PRAISE FOR *THIRTY MINUTES: CHANGED FOREVER*

"While the subject matter is disturbing, I couldn't put this book down! Julie M. Frawley gives us a privileged glimpse inside the mind and heart of a person who has undergone trauma and is wrestling with those questions that we all feel when evil happens. But the end result is another privileged glimpse into a person who has been forever changed by the transforming power of forgiveness."

- Fr. John Riccardo, pastor, Our Lady of Good Counsel

"Ms. Frawley has produced a book that can be an important tool, in different ways, for several different groups of people who have been touched by sexual assault. This book can be a tool for victims of sexual assault. The author's frank description of her thoughts, feelings, and reactions on her journey toward recovery can confirm for another victim that whatever they are feeling is valid, no matter how unexpected and out of control the feelings may seem. It can also confirm that recovery is possible.

"This book can be a tool for the families and loved ones of a victim of sexual assault. The insight into what their loved one may continue to experience after the assault and throughout recovery can be invaluable. This book can be a tool for Police Investigators and Prosecuting Attorneys. By having a fuller understanding of what a victim of sexual assault has gone through, an investigator and a prosecutor can approach and deal with future victims in ways that gain the trust and cooperation that will facilitate the arrest and conviction of the offender."

- Retired Detective Mary Timmons Fairman, Oak Park Police

"Most books about crimes and the criminal justice system are written from the viewpoint of a detective, forensic scientist, lawyer, or defendant. *Thirty Minutes* corrects this omission, and provides the reader with a rare glimpse into the world of the crime victim. Frawley's book is the very personal story of one woman's struggle for survival and healing, and reminds us that crime stories don't end with a verdict or a sentence. For the victim of a violent crime these events provide merely the setting for an emotional struggle which lasts a lifetime."

- Brian Zubel, attorney and forensic science legal consultant, specially appointed assistant prosecutor for Berrien County, and specially appointed associate examiner for the Michigan Judicial Tenure Commission

"*Thirty Minutes: Changed Forever* is a factual account of a horrific life-altering rape. Frawley paints a realistic picture of the emotional roller coaster she has experienced then and now. An accurate portrayal of how the system at times works or doesn't work. Even after all these years, we still have a long way to go to ensure that all sexual assault survivors are treated with the respect and dignity that they deserve."

- Beth Morrison, president/CEO, HAVEN

"From the fabric of life, the author shares her own personal, traumatic story which changed her life's direction. Interwoven within its pages you will experience the pain, isolation, and fear which at times immobilized her. However, accompanying her into her valley of despair, you will also experience the constant presence and love of God for her, and the redeeming forgiveness which ultimately liberates her from being a victim to become a victor. Powerful! Insightful! Inspiring!"

- Tom Bruno, psychologist

THIRTY MINUTES

Changed Forever

Julie M. Frawley

FERNE PRESS

Summary: The true story of a rape and the twenty years of healing and spiritual growth that followed.

Isaiah 42:16 is taken from the New American Bible, St. Joseph Edition © 1970. Confraternity of Christian Doctrine, Washington D.C., Catholic Book Publishing Co., New York, N.Y.

Library of Congress Cataloging-in-Publication Data
Frawley, Julie M. (1960 –)
Thirty Minutes: Changed Forever / Julie M. Frawley
– First Edition
ISBN# 9781933916118

1. Rape 2. Christian 3. Non-fiction 4. True crime 5. Self-help
6. Reference
I. Frawley, Julie M. II. Thirty Minutes: Changed Forever
Library of Congress Control Number: 2007938954

FERNE PRESS

Ferne Press is an imprint of Nelson Publishing & Marketing
366 Welch Road, Northville, MI 48167
www.nelsonpublishingandmarketing.com
(248) 735-0418

This is a true story. The name of the perpetrator and some other names in this book have been changed to protect the privacy of the victims. Permission has been granted to include the names of some real individuals.

Courtroom dialogue has been taken from the records of the following Michigan courts: Berkley 45A District Court, Royal Oak 44th District Court, and Circuit Court for the Sixth Judicial Circuit of Michigan. Court references do not include case numbers in order to protect the privacy of the victims. Courtroom dialogue has been edited for readability.

Dedicated to my dad, who through his own loving nature, helped me to recognize and experience the love of God the Father

I will lead the blind on their journey; by paths unknown I will guide them. I will turn darkness into light before them, and make crooked ways straight. These things I do for them, and I will not forsake them.

Isaiah 42:16

CONTENTS

PART TWO: CHANGED FOREVER

FOREWORD

Since 1965, I have met, interviewed, and counseled thousands of victims of rape and violence. No one has touched and impressed me more than Julie Frawley.

I remember our first meeting in 1986 when her mother, who was one of my students, introduced her to my university class. Julie was not ashamed as she vividly recalled the horrors of that awful morning. Julie was not a silhouette, but the face of a real rape victim that so many have never seen. She was not afraid to challenge the criminal justice system and support others hurt by this devastating crime. Since that day, many others have heard Julie's message as a victim, an educator, a mother, a daughter, and a friend.

Thirty Minutes: Changed Forever graphically tells of Julie Frawley's life and spiritual growth, which are the qualities that make her story so special and make Julie such an inspiring person. You will cry, you will get angry, but her story is real life, and by the time you finish, you will care deeply about Julie and everyone else who has been violated by rape. Her common, yet tenacious touch will inspire others not to be silent victims.

Thirty Minutes: Changed Forever is an important book that should be read by men and women alike. I am honored to have been asked to write this forward.

Isaiah McKinnon, Ph.D.
University of Detroit Mercy - Department of Education
Retired Chief of Police, City of Detroit

ABOUT IKE MCKINNON

Dr. Isaiah "Ike" McKinnon is known and admired by the citizens of Detroit, Michigan as an experienced educator and loyal public servant. He was appointed chief of police in 1994, and served four years, during which time he created special police units and task forces that reduced violent crimes. To that position, he brought his years of experience in various capacities within the Detroit Police Department, including lieutenant in charge of the sex crime unit and adjunct professor of criminal justice at various colleges and universities.

After retiring as chief of police in 1998, McKinnon joined the faculty at University of Detroit Mercy, where he currently teaches courses in education and teacher development. He also formed the "McKinnon Group," a company that specializes in diversity training, motivational speaking, and professional consulting. In addition, he is the safety consultant/expert at WDIV-TV, Channel 4, in Detroit.

McKinnon is the author of *Stand Tall, In the Line of Duty,* and *North Between the Houses.* He has received numerous awards, including the NAACP Image Award, the Catholic Youth Organization Award for "Positive Influence on Community," recognition from the Michigan State Senate for "Touching the Lives of Countless People," and an Emmy Award for his WDIV-TV Program *Stay Safe with Ike.*

INTRODUCTION

On August 29, 1986, at age twenty-six, I was brutally raped in my own home. The rape lasted less than half an hour. Yet, those thirty minutes have impacted every day of my life since the incident occurred.

In the weeks that followed, I longed for the sense of security that I once had. At night, I prayed that the next morning would bring relief from the extreme terror that I was experiencing. It didn't happen.

I was angry with God. *How could He allow this to happen to me?* Although I didn't trust God, I couldn't stop thinking about Him. My anger repelled me from Him, yet it also drew me closer to Him.

This book is not just about that one day in my life—it is also about the twenty years of healing and spiritual growth that followed. It is about my need to talk about it still after all this time. If more people understand the humiliation and feelings of violation that occur during a sexual assault, friends, neighbors, and family members won't continue to say:

At least he didn't hurt you.

I told the police that you were a good girl.

Your fears are irrational.

Can't you just forget about it?

By sharing the story of my rape, my sincere hope is that others might benefit from the insights I have learned throughout my long recovery.

PART ONE

THIRTY MINUTES

ONE

Single, Content, and Excited About the Future

The gag in my mouth kept me from speaking clearly. Breathing took all my strength. It seemed as if the two-hundred-pound brute lying on top of me was fumbling with something behind my back. I thought he was taking a gun or a knife out of his pocket, preparing to kill me. I heard a loud click. I assumed he was opening a switchblade.

I braced myself for the pain I would feel from a knife plunging into my back or from a bullet exploding in my head.

For the first twenty-six years of my life, I was a proper Catholic girl. My parents sent me to a private Catholic school from grade school through high school. Religion was more of a duty than an inspiration. I prayed the prayers that were written by others, but I don't remember many conversations with God. When I thought about Him, I felt fear, not love. He watched over us in order to catch us making a mistake, and then He punished us.

Death frightened me—the thought of someone I loved dying made me unbearably anxious, and I would immediately erase the thought from my mind. Years later, I would be shocked at the thoughts that actually did

1

go through my mind when I was faced with the real possibility of my life ending.

———————————

In August 1986, I had just celebrated my twenty-sixth birthday. I had a new job with a business and technology services firm in Detroit, Michigan. It was the beginning of a promising career for me. I was living in the small home I had purchased in the well-kept, and thriving suburban city of Royal Oak. The community was considered safe and the neighbors were a close-knit group.

Purchasing a home on my own was a major goal that I had set for myself, and I was proud of my accomplishment. My new home was an adorable, two-bedroom bungalow on a quiet street. It was a white, aluminum-sided house with an old-fashioned metal awning covering the front porch. In my eyes, it was perfect, although in reality it needed some tender loving care. With the help of my parents, I spent a great deal of time renovating each room. The changes that we made to this 1948 home created a warm and inviting atmosphere. I was comfortable there, and believed it would bring me many years of happiness.

The neighbors were especially kind. George was an elderly man who lived next door with his wife, Sarah, who suffered from arthritis. George was so busy caring for her and helping other people that he didn't always take time to care for his own property. His yard was filled with many unusual treasures. He would often comment that the only thing holding up the roof on his garage was the junk inside. Often, on winter mornings, before I had a chance to grab my own snow shovel, I would hear George's snow blower clearing my sidewalks. This man treated me as if I was his own daughter. In the summer, George and I talked over the chain-link fence, and often other neighbors would join us. Adding to my sense of security, the family across the street had a large Doberman pinscher that paced the sidewalk in front of their house, as if guarding a palace.

Completing my bachelor's degree was another goal, and I was attending Oakland University part-time. I was also taking classes through work that would allow me to advance to a better position.

Joanne, a close childhood friend, was my roommate in my new home. Her cat, Brandy, also lived with us. Frequently, new acquaintances mistook us for sisters. Joanne and I shared many friends who would visit us often. Bernadette was one of these treasured friends, although I saw her less regularly since she had gotten married and had a daughter. My boyfriend, Gary, whom I loved, had recently moved to Florida. We were maintaining a long-distance relationship. I missed him, and we talked on the phone a lot.

It was a busy time in my life and I was incredibly self-absorbed. With a feeling of being invincible, I paid little attention to my surroundings as I rushed to and from work and school. My youth and inexperience led me to believe that I had complete control over everything I did and everything that happened to me. The thought of anything stopping me or interfering with my life's plans never occurred to me. This is why I did not take seriously the warning signs that someone was about to turn my life upside down.

TWO

WARNING SIGNS

My house was on a corner lot. I did not have a garage, but there was a driveway and parking pad on the side street behind the house. Joanne and I would park our cars in the driveway, then walk along the side of the house and around to the front door. This made Joanne nervous at night, and she often reminded me that the backyard needed some lighting. The possibility of anything going wrong never occurred to me, so I never did buy the light that Joanne had urged me to install.

I was working the afternoon shift one warm, summer night in July, when Joanne called me at work and said that she heard strange noises in our backyard, outside of her bedroom window. She believed that someone was in the yard, looking through the window at her. I suggested that it was her imagination. Her fear was so intense that she called a friend and asked her to spend the evening with her.

During the early part of August, I realized that someone had been in my car during the night while it was parked in the driveway. Several items were moved from where I had left them. Later, I discovered that my cassette tapes were missing. I was only briefly frightened that a stranger had been rummaging through my car.

Another day I noticed that a cinder block had been moved from the side of the house to the back of the house, beneath Joanne's bedroom window. It is embarrassing to admit that I ignored all of these red flags and did not worry a lot about these incidents. In fact, I did not even mention them to Gary during our phone conversations. In retrospect, it appears that Joanne and I were being watched by a stalker for several weeks, or possibly even months. At the time, it was more comfortable for me to disregard these danger signs and feel safe, rather than to allow myself to become fearful.

Finally, on August 17, my sleep was interrupted in the early morning by a phone call. Looking at my alarm clock, I noticed it was five thirty-seven. When I answered, there was silence at first, so I hung up the receiver. Although I am not sure why, I picked up the phone again after a few seconds, and I heard a male voice that I did not recognize say my name. He spoke slowly, in an eerie whisper, and then there was more silence. *How does he know that it is me answering the phone and not my roommate?* My heart beat faster as I hung up the phone, wondering who would want to frighten me. To my horror, it rang again a couple of minutes later. My hand was now shaking as I lifted the receiver. This time, no one spoke on the other end of the line.

For the next two weeks, I would be alone in my house. Joanne had promised her parents that she would stay at their home and care for their dogs while they were on vacation. Brandy, Joanne's cat, would stay home with me. Although I was normally too stubborn to ask for help, my fear was now so intense that I decided to ask several family members to take turns sleeping at my house for the next few days. By the fifth day, there had been no more calls, and I talked myself into believing that I was over-reacting. No threats had been made, so what was I worried about? Also, having other people staying with me was making it difficult to focus on my studies, so I stayed alone, and felt safe.

My parents, however, were still concerned. One day my dad pulled me aside and had a conversation with me about guns. He had asked me if I would consider owning a gun to keep in our home for protection. I rejected the idea, saying that even if someone did break in and threaten my life, I would never be able to shoot another person.

Twelve days had passed since I received the bizarre, early morning phone calls. The stress of working long hours was taking its toll on me and I had little time for anything other than my studies. I had spoken to Gary only one time throughout these two weeks, and never brought up the subject of the phone calls. It was August 29, a Friday morning, the day before Labor Day weekend. Sleeping peacefully in my room, I was unaware of the danger that awaited me. The nightmare I was about to experience would be one from which I could not wake up. A stranger, a predator, was hiding in the next room, waiting silently in the closet—waiting to execute his premeditated attack.

THREE

The Nightmare Begins

The buzzing of my alarm clock woke me at seven twenty a.m. It was the final day of the intensive two-week training class for work. This was the day I had looked forward to since I joined this company. The previous two weeks had been exhausting, spent writing and decoding computer programs at an off-site training facility. One more day, and I would be done with the training requirements. Then I could enjoy Labor Day weekend, and attend my family's annual reunion before returning to my regular job. Moving slowly, I took the time to make my bed. While choosing the clothes I would wear that day, I noticed that it was incredibly hot in the house. Wandering out of my bedroom and into the living room, I glanced at the thermostat. Eighty degrees! My heat had been turned off all summer, and I had not touched the thermostat in months.

My thoughts flashed back to the previous night. It had been an especially cool evening for August. Instead of pajamas, I had worn a purple sweatshirt and sweatpants to bed for warmth. I knew that I had closed all of the windows in the house before going to sleep, and I even remembered removing the fan in Joanne's bedroom window and pulling the window shut. My eyes quickly glanced towards her room.

There was a clear view of her window and the fan that I had removed the night before. But to my surprise, the fan was in a different position than I had left it, and the window I had closed was now wide open! Walking over to Joanne's bedroom door, I thought, *Joanne must have come home during the night and turned on the heat. But why would the window be open now?* Unafraid, I glanced inside her room. The bed was made, but her normally tidy room looked as if a tornado had passed through it. Dresser drawers were strewn open, and tangled masses of clothing were hanging out of them.

Remarkably, I still was not frightened. *What terrible emergency caused Joanne to come home and pack up her clothes with such carelessness? How is it possible that she didn't wake me up?* I had been awake less than ten minutes, and my thoughts were still somewhat fuzzy. Thinking that I must be dreaming, I tried to rub the sleep out of my eyes.

Suddenly, I was catapulted into the middle of a horror movie. Without warning, the door to her closet flew open! Before I could blink, a tall, husky form with a nylon stocking pulled over his face lunged toward me. My lungs wanted air, and as I gasped for breath, every muscle in my body froze. The intruder's distorted, grotesque face was less than a foot from mine as this six-foot, tall monster shoved me backwards into the living room.

"What are you doing here!" I heard myself shriek as he threw me to the floor at the base of my grandfather clock. My screams continued to fill the air.

Without hesitation, the intruder answered my question in an angry voice. "You caught me ripping off your house!" His right hand reached around my head and he shoved a wadded-up rag of some sort into my mouth with such force that I began choking. In my mind I kept crying the same two words over and over: *Wake up! Wake up! Wake up! This can't really be happening to me. It must be a nightmare, but why can't I wake up?*

The unexpected ambush of this dark figure bolting from the closet allowed him to take complete control over me. I had always considered myself to be physically strong, but because of his surprise tactic, there was no time to think or even react. I was incapable of putting up any kind of struggle.

The intruder was an incredibly strong man, and he was able to flip over my one hundred twenty-five-pound body with little effort. I was still paralyzed with fear when he held both my wrists together behind my back and expertly whipped some kind of cord around them as if he had done this many times before.

The sight of this man as he pushed me backwards etched a permanent image in my brain. His sweatshirt and sweatpants were navy blue, and his pockets were bulging. During our struggle, I noticed several small stuffed animals, apparently in his possession, go sailing through the air and onto the carpet. *Are they the stuffed animals that normally adorn Joanne's bed?*

As I lay on the floor, the weight of this two-hundred-pound brute was crushing my legs. Face down, my nose and mouth buried in the carpet, I was gagging with the pressure of the cloth on the back of my throat. My tears added to this torture. It was almost impossible for me to catch my breath and I started to choke.

To my horror, the intruder then reached around my head and pinched my nostrils shut with his thumb and forefinger. I could no longer breathe! Again, I heard his hateful voice. "This is what will happen if you don't stop crying!"

It was unclear if this was a serious threat or if he was telling me that I needed to calm down so I wouldn't suffocate. Somehow, I was able to gain enough control over myself to stop crying. If I angered him, I reasoned, he would become more vicious. He let go of my nose.

My thoughts raced in a desperate attempt to figure out how to escape. *He won't get off my legs or allow me to move. I have no control over what this man is doing to me. Why doesn't he just take what he wants and leave me alone? Is he enjoying watching me suffer?* The gag in my mouth prevented me from speaking clearly. Breathing took all of my strength. At that moment, surviving was all that mattered.

The next few minutes seemed like an eternity. It appeared as if he was fumbling with something behind my back. Since I was unable to see what he was doing, I thought that he was preparing to kill me. *Is he struggling to take a gun or a knife out of his pocket?* Lying face down, I could only speculate. It was agonizing. Then I heard the sound of a loud click that I assumed was a switchblade being opened.

I braced myself for the pain I would feel from a knife plunging into my back or from a bullet exploding in my head. This intense fright was paralyzing. It seemed as though time stood still, but my mind went on fighting the idea that this was really happening. *How can another human being continue to inflict pain on someone who is bound and helpless? Why does a man want to hurt a woman he doesn't even know? Why did he choose me?* The stabbing I was expecting did not come. Instead a strange thing happened. A quiet peace came over me—a sudden, overwhelming sense that I was being comforted. It was as though I was shielded from this horrendous fright. Although I hadn't thought to call on God for help, I believe He came anyway. This peaceful presence was in sharp contrast to the storm that raged around me. My lifelong fear of dying seemed to disappear.

My thoughts calmly turned to my family. I was concerned with how they would be able to handle the sight of my lifeless body when they walked into my house. Suddenly, it became very important for me to die face up, rather than in the face-down position that I was being held in. I can't explain this feeling, but it was intense. Perhaps I wanted him to see me as a person instead of prey. *If he looks into my eyes, will it change the outcome?* As I struggled to turn over, my captor became even more hostile.

FOUR

Rape!

Because his first words to me were, "You caught me ripping off your house," it had not occurred to me that he might have broken into my home for any reason other than burglary. I assumed that he was angry with me for catching him, and now he was going to teach me a lesson.

As I struggled to free my hands, the pain in my tightly bound wrists worsened. The peace that I experienced was now eclipsed by my physical pain. Despair diminished my ability to think clearly. If God was speaking to me now, I couldn't hear what He was saying. I struggled to think of words that would convince the intruder to leave, but it was futile. As I mentally prepared to die, I felt his hand grab the elastic waistband of my sweatpants. Slowly and deliberately, he dragged the sweatpants down to my ankles, and then pulled them off of my body entirely.

A scream erupted from somewhere deep inside of me. It began as a slow and violent tremble that traveled through every inch of my body. As I cried out in anguish, I prayed for God to take me. For the first time, it was clear to me that this man had invaded my home for the purpose of raping me. He was not going to stop, and all of my physical strength and power could not prevent this violation from happening. He had complete control over me. *Please help me God. Make him stop!*

He continued undressing me as if I was a mannequin, pulling my underwear off next. The thought of him staring at my body was unbearable. Through my gag, I tried pleading in muffled cries for him to stop. I

13

remembered that I had my period and thought that telling him might stop him or slow him down. *What will happen if he rapes me with a tampon in place?*

Somehow he was able to understand my anguished pleas, but instead of abandoning his plans, he calmly responded, "That's all right." Laying face down, with my hands tied behind me, I felt this stranger pull out the tampon that should only have been removed by me.

In one swift motion, every ounce of my dignity was stripped away. Of all the acts that he committed against me that morning, removing my tampon left the deepest scar. It created a wound that has never healed. Later that morning, the tampon would be seen on the living room carpet by every neighbor and police officer that entered my house.

I kept praying that someone would hear my screams or that I would somehow figure out a way to free my hands. At this point, the rapist took a long pause, during which I could hear the heaviness of his breathing. Lying on the carpet in anticipation of the next horror that awaited me was agonizing. Even if he didn't physically kill me, I was dying inside.

Suddenly, my thoughts drifted back to my family and peaceful memories, in which I could see their familiar faces. I thought of how much I loved them and wished that I could tell them. My prayers focused on them, and I worried about the impact my death would have on them. My thoughts were interrupted by the physical touch of my attacker, and the nightmare continued. The remainder of the time that he was in my house, I would go back and forth from thoughts of my parents to the realization that I was being raped.

The rapist turned my body over so I was facing him. The stocking was over his head the entire time, although he would occasionally lift it up, exposing his mouth. He was careful not to let me see the rest of his face. In control and determined, he proceeded with his torturous agenda. It seemed as though his step-by-step plan was designed to degrade and humiliate me. It involved the invasion of many parts of my body, as he performed a variety of acts, all sexual in nature. He expected little from me except that I lie there and keep quiet. Amid the sounds of my choking and gagging on the rag jammed in my mouth, he performed oral sex on me. I struggled to control my nausea. *What kind of a man can perform oral sex on a woman during her period?* Then he lifted my sweatshirt and roughly put his mouth on my left breast. He sadistically enjoyed my suffering, and I could sense the anger that was driving him.

Handling my body as if I were already dead, he rolled me back over so I was facing the floor again. My wrists were in pain but I knew there was no point in asking him to untie them. It was as though I was an object instead of a person. He seemed to thrive on my anguish, and I was a victim to his whims.

Although my face was buried in the carpet, I could sense that he was searching for something in his pockets again. Once again I began to panic, believing he was searching for a gun. He must have known what I was thinking because he put a small plastic bottle into my hands and smugly said, "This is what I have." He then took the bottle, opened it, and poured some type of lotion onto the palms of my tied hands.

With my head turned to the side, I could see him pull the navy-blue sweatpants that he was wearing down to his knees. He leaned over my body and began to rub his penis against my bound hands. I remember hoping he would hurry up and ejaculate so he would be done with me and leave me alone. It soon became clear that he was not finished.

He positioned himself on top of me, so I was pinned down with more weight than I had previously felt. A feeling of panic swept through me as I braced myself for his next move. A stabbing pain tore through my body as he attempted to penetrate my anus with his penis. The pressure was tremendous and I began screaming again. My fear was that this pain was going to be more than I could endure. My reaction seemed to fuel his anger and he yelled at me to "Shut up!" and "Be quiet!" The tension in my body would not allow him to enter me. Thankfully, he became discouraged and stopped trying.

It was at this moment that I heard what appeared to be a car door slamming outside of my house. A glimmer of hope! The sound was close and I wondered if Joanne had decided to stop home before driving into work that morning from her parent's house.

"Someone's here!" were the muffled words that burst from my mouth.

Apparently, my attacker heard the noise too.

"It's probably just your roommate" was his calm reply, as if he was expecting her. *Is he hoping that Joanne will walk through the door?* A new fear invaded my thoughts. *Will she become my rescuer? Or his next victim?* We waited in silence, both wondering if we would hear the jingle of keys as she attempted to unlock the front door. The sound never came. We were still alone.

Showing no sign of frustration, he continued his abuse. Only a few seconds passed before I felt his hand between my legs and his fingers force their way inside of me. Frantically, I tried to squirm away in anticipation of the next strike, but his strength was overwhelming. He used his penis as the weapon for his torture, and his subsequent attempts at penetration were successful.

Still face down on the carpet, I prayed for him to finish. With my head turned to the side, I was able to see his left hand positioned on the floor next to my head. For the first time, I noticed that he was wearing white latex gloves. The skin on his index finger and thumb was exposed because the fingers of the glove had been cut off. My assailant was fair-skinned and had short, neatly trimmed fingernails. I was confused as to the reason the fingers were cut off the glove, but assumed it was for the purpose of touching me.

It wasn't long before his breathing slowed and he leaned back, away from my body, and said, "That wasn't so bad, was it?"

Tears were my only response.

With my head turned sideways, I was able to watch him out of the corner of my eye. He stood up, pulled his sweatpants back on, and began rustling with the items in his pockets again. My body was trembling as I attempted to face him once more, but with clenched teeth he yelled at me to turn over. During the rape, I had been numb to all but the most extreme physical pain. The psychological pain had been far greater. However, I was slowly becoming more aware of the throbbing in my wrists. When I asked him to untie them, he blurted out, "You can untie them when I leave." *He is going to leave!* For the first time, I realized that he did not intend to kill me. The entire time that he was raping me, I believed that my life was going to end.

I sensed a shift in his demeanor. Apparently he was done with me. As he turned and walked into my kitchen, I watched him closely. His actions were hurried as he leaned over my kitchen table and peered out the window that faced the front of the house. I assumed that he was looking for a way out, but first wanted to make sure the neighbors wouldn't see him leave. My body stiffened, and I turned my head away as he walked back into the living room where I was still laying face down on the carpet. I did not want him to know that I was watching him. It was my belief that my life would still be in danger if he thought that I could recognize him.

He walked past the spot where I was lying, moving toward the front door. I then saw him grab the doorknob. For the first time, he appeared nervous as he struggled to let himself out. It seemed like an eternity before he was finally able to open the door. As I watched from behind, I saw him pull the stocking off of his head. His dark brown, short, wavy hair was now visible. He then walked out of my house, pulling the door shut behind him. A sense of relief unlike anything I had ever felt swept through me.

Somehow I managed to stand up and run to my kitchen window to reassure myself that he had really left. It was then that I saw the profile of this large man with full cheeks dart across my front lawn. Oblivious to my physical pain, I ran from room to room, watching out each window, as he nervously jogged down the street that ran along the side of my house. When he disappeared down a side street behind my house, I took a deep breath and caught sight of my own reflection in the window. My distorted face startled me. My medium-length, dark-brown hair was a tangled mess. Tears were streaming down my cheeks. My arms, bound by the cord, were pulled tightly behind my back, and I was still naked from the waist down. For a moment, I stared at myself in amazement. I was alive!

Running to my telephone, I knocked the receiver off its cradle with my chin. It fell to the floor. Struggling to get down on my knees, I was able to put my ear to the receiver. When I heard no dial tone I was puzzled, and then realized that my phone line had been cut. A feeling of panic momentarily gripped me. I would have to leave my house in order to call the police.

FIVE

An Angel in Uniform

S till frantic, I looked around for my sweatpants and saw them lying on the carpet near the front door. Although my hands were still tied behind my back, I picked them up with my teeth and hastily straightened them out on the floor. I was then able to sit down and work my legs into them. Finally I was able to grasp the elastic waistband with my bound hands behind me and pull them up. My sweatshirt had never been completely removed but had fallen back into place after it had been lifted by my attacker. At some point I was able to spit out the gag from my mouth, although I don't remember doing this.

My body was trembling uncontrollably. In a state of shock, I couldn't believe that I not only survived the attack, but had experienced an amazing transformation in the midst of it. A message had been relayed to me suddenly and clearly: *There is no need to fear death. If your life is taken, you will be all right. Your body can be harmed, but your spirit cannot be touched.* These words were not spoken aloud—they were imprinted on my soul.

I backed up to my front door and struggled to turn the doorknob. After several bungled tries, it finally opened. Ironically, it was the same door my attacker had used to gain his freedom. Instinctively, I ran in the direction of George's house. Breathing heavily, I darted across my lawn and around the fence that separated our homes. I frantically leaned against his doorbell and kicked at his outside door to get his attention. I was sobbing uncontrollably. It was still early, about eight o'clock, but he quickly came to the door. He seemed to assess the situation quickly, and I can still remember the horrified look on his face. With trembling hands, he used his pocketknife to cut the cord that still bound my wrists. I regretted subjecting him to that trauma.

I lied, telling him only that my house had been robbed. George immediately led me into his living room and called the police. Sarah, his wife, was sitting silently at the dining room table. Putting down the receiver, George told her to stay with me, and dashed out the door, heading towards my house. My heart sank because I knew that when George entered my house, my violation would scream out to him. He would see my underwear and the tampon that the rapist had pulled from me, lying on the living room carpet. As I lost sight of George, I felt any dignity that I had left slip away.

Slowly, I turned toward Sarah. A half-eaten piece of toast was on the plate in front of her. It appeared that they were in the middle of breakfast when I interrupted them. Sarah, a petite, gray-haired woman, appeared to be a few years older than her active husband. Because of her arthritis she rarely ventured out of the house. She calmly told me that I could use their phone to call anyone I needed.

I thanked Sarah and picked up the receiver. As I struggled to remember my own mother's telephone number, I wondered, *What will I tell her when she answers?* Mentally, I rehearsed the words that I would use when she picked up the receiver. I didn't want her to panic. My worry was in vain. No one answered the phone.

Even though Sarah was with me, I felt alone and helpless. Blinking my eyes, I attempted to see through the tears that kept forming and picked up the phone again. Trembling, I carried it into the kitchen and turned away from Sarah to prevent her from hearing me talk. This time I dialed the number to the office where I worked. If I didn't show up on this last day of class, I would lose my job. My boss was not expecting me in the Detroit office, but he might be getting a phone call that would let him know that I did not show up for the last day of training.

Lisa, a friend and coworker, was working the first shift that morning and answered the phone. It would be much easier to tell her what had happened than to explain it to someone else. By now I had managed to compose myself and could talk calmly. In a hushed voice, I told her what had happened to me, and I asked her to tell Jeff, our manager. Lisa's voice was quivering as she assured me that she would notify him.

Next, I called Joanne at her parent's house. She hadn't left for work yet. I dreaded telling her what happened—my house was her home as well. When she answered, I explained that our house had been broken into during the night, but nothing was taken. I let her know that I had tried to call my mom but was unable to reach her. Although she seemed confused, Joanne offered to continue calling my mom's house until she answered. My parents did not have an answering machine at the time.

The police arrived at my house within three minutes of George's phone call. Later, he led one of the police officers to his house, where I was now sitting with Sarah at the dining room table. Through the window, I watched the male police officer climb the steps to George's porch. I waited for the front door to open. When it did, our eyes met, and I was struck by the officer's apparent youth. His hair was a medium-brown color and his expression was soft and kind. He motioned for me to come out onto the porch. Calmly, he asked if we could go back to my house to talk about what happened.

The officer walked me slowly back to the house I had fled from only twenty minutes earlier. Numerous police cars lined the street, and I sensed that my neighbors were staring at me from their front windows. As we walked around the fence that divided our houses, I saw Joanne's boyfriend, Sean, walking across the lawn from the direction of his parked car. Joanne must have sent him to our house after she hung up with me. It was a relief when I saw his familiar face approaching me. No words were spoken, but I could tell by the look on his face when our eyes met that he knew what had happened. Sean's hug was a comfort to me.

The police officer continued walking with me toward my house. As we approached the porch, I hesitated. Visions of the nightmare that had occurred flashed through my mind. I preferred to talk outside, although I said nothing, and reluctantly I followed him into my house. As I walked up the concrete steps toward the door, my heart began to race. The police officer held the front door open for me, and slowly I stepped into my living room. Sean was asked to wait on the front porch.

Walking through my living room, my eyes quickly scanned the beige carpet where I was assaulted. It appeared as though the police had removed all of the evidence that had been left on the floor. Looking toward the back hallway near the bedrooms, I saw several of Joanne's stuffed animals lying on the carpet. I remembered the feeling of terror as the intruder pushed me backwards into the living room. Inside her room, Joanne's fan had been left on the floor, and I suddenly noticed that the cord had been cut from it. Then I remembered the clicking sound I heard after my captor had bound my hands. *He must have cut the cord with a knife and used it to tie my wrists. Maybe the clicking noise was the sound of the knife being closed.* Quickly, I turned my head and shut my eyes.

My next memory is of this soft-spoken policeman offering me a seat at my own kitchen table. Even though I was trembling and still dazed, I noticed the concerned look of compassion on his face, as if he were holding back tears. Immediately I felt comfortable with this man.

He told me that his name was Officer Mike Struble and asked if there was anything he could get for me. Then he sat down on the kitchen chair next to me and turned so his eyes were looking into mine. My crying didn't seem to bother him. He waited patiently until I was able to compose myself. Officer Struble then calmly asked me to explain what had happened.

"I was raped," I said quietly.

His expression never changed. Those same compassionate eyes continued looking directly into mine. He already knew.

Tearfully, I explained to Officer Struble that I needed to take a shower. I felt contaminated and wanted to remove all traces of the rapist from my body. He suggested that I wait, saying it would hurt their investigation if I washed away important evidence. Reluctantly, I agreed.

Instinctively, I trusted this policeman and told him everything I could remember about the assault. It was clear that if I gave him a detailed description of the intruder, it would be easier to catch him and stop him from raping others. Officer Struble gave me complete control over the interview, something I desperately needed while feeling that everything else was out of control. He never lost eye contact with me or asked me to stop crying. Nor did he imply that I was responsible in any way for what had happened to me. As a result of his compassionate approach, I was not ashamed of being raped. I learned that I could talk about the details of this crime without feeling embarrassed or humiliated. This attitude has never left me. In my eyes, this policeman was an angel sent from heaven. The dignity and respect with which he treated me during that interview helped me to form a solid foundation on which to begin my recovery.

Although I was vaguely aware that other people were now in my house collecting evidence, I focused only on Officer Struble. As I spoke, he listened intently and took copious notes. He seemed to be writing down most of what I said, stopping me occasionally to ask me to expand on my description of my attacker. When he finished his questions, he stayed seated. Then he shared with me that someone close to him had also been a victim of a rapist. As a result, he was deeply affected by each rape victim that he interviewed.

At some point during our conversation, I was told that Joanne had arrived at our house. This filled me with a tremendous sense of relief. To my dismay, the police officer on the front porch refused to let her in. A hug from her might have helped me cope.

Shortly after I finished talking to Officer Struble, an older woman with short, dark hair walked through my front door. She wore glasses and a navy-blue blazer, and the look on her face suggested she was all business. As she turned toward the kitchen, Officer Struble saw her and stood up. When she nodded her head in his direction, he responded by saying, "Hello, Detective."

The dining area of my kitchen wasn't much bigger than the table that was in it, so the officer moved into the living room to allow the detective to enter. Her face was expressionless as she introduced herself as Detective Shanahan. Missing was the look of compassion I found so comforting on the face of Officer Strubel.

Still seated at my kitchen table, I was forced to look up at the detective *standing* over me. When Officer Strubel had *sat down* next to me, it had put me at ease. In an attempt to avoid a conversation with her, I told her that I had already given a statement to the police officer.

"I'll need you to tell me, too," responded the detective sternly. Tears filled my eyes as I began talking. Once again I had to tell about being attacked, having my hands tied behind my back, and what he did to me. Talking about this for the second time was unbearable, and it intensified the need I felt to take a shower.

Detective Shanahan appeared annoyed with the way I was responding to her questions. Perhaps it was my crying, or I hadn't given her enough details, but she ordered me to "calm down" several times during our conversation. I felt betrayed by this woman, whom I expected to be supportive. She dominated our conversation, in contrast to Officer Struble, who had allowed me to take my time and regain some of the control that I had lost.

After what seemed like hours, the detective announced that she was through with her questions. As she stood up and turned toward my living room, I heard the familiar sound of the screen door being opened. Slowly, I stood up with the intention of walking toward my living room. I felt light-headed and steadied myself by gripping the back of the chair I had been sitting in for so long. Detective Shanahan was now speaking to the person who had just entered my house. My view of this new arrival was blocked by the open front door. As I moved closer to my living room, I heard a familiar voice tearfully respond to Detective Shanahan, "I'm her mother." Then I saw her. The anguish in my mother's eyes startled me. Her mouth opened as she stared at me, but she said nothing. I waited to hear the words that had gotten lodged in her throat. Cautiously, she approached me with her arms outstretched. She hugged me as if she thought I might break. We were both crying. No words were exchanged, nor did they seem necessary.

Moments later I felt the soft touch of someone's hand on my shoulder. When I turned my head, I saw Officer Struble standing beside me. He suggested that my mother and I have a seat on the couch in the living room. Obediently, I walked through the living room, being careful to avoid the exact spot on the carpet where the rape had occurred. Mom sat down, as directed. I chose to remain standing, unable to relax after my talk with Detective Shanahan. I caught a glimpse of the clock. *Is it really ten fifteen? The police officers have been in my house for over two hours!*

Throughout the entire morning, I was having trouble focusing on anything other than the conversation I was involved in at the time. Everything that was happening around me was a blur. I had been unaware of the time, or that Officer Struble was still in my house while Detective Shanahan was speaking to me.

Officer Struble looked as if he had something to tell us, although he seemed somewhat hesitant at first. He then explained that if the police found the man who had attacked me, they would need physical evidence to prove that he was guilty. The best way to collect it was for me to go to the hospital and request that a rape kit be used during my exam. He explained that I could make the choice of whether or not I would go to the hospital. No one would force me.

Unfamiliar with the term *rape kit,* I was puzzled. Briefly, Officer Struble described the procedure that would be performed by the hospital. The nurse would take blood and hair samples from me. They would also clip the tips off my fingernails. In the event that I had been able to scratch the perpetrator, his skin cells might be found under my nails. A pelvic exam would also be done by the doctor to collect any semen left during the rape. These tests could provide the authorities with a sample of the rapist's DNA, allowing them to match it with a blood sample from the perpetrator. The thought of having this procedure done was upsetting. Now my anger was beginning to surface. As a result of what he did to me, I needed to allow myself to be probed and prodded in an emergency room!

Surprisingly, this anger felt good. Maybe it would provide me with the strength I needed to make it through the hospital procedures. There was no question in my mind that I would do whatever it took to catch the man who raped me.

Officer Struble began speaking to my mother again. He needed to know which hospital she would be taking me to in order to notify the emergency room that we were on our way. My mother, a registered nurse, suggested that we go to the hospital where she was employed. Officer Struble advised me to take a change of clothes with me. The hospital would be keeping the ones that I was wearing as evidence. Then he walked out the front door to make the phone call to the hospital.

Obediently, I walked back through the hallway in the rear of the house where my bedroom was located. Pausing outside of Joanne's bedroom, I looked in and noticed her window was still open. Several of her stuffed animals that had been in the pockets of the rapist were lying on the floor near my feet. It seemed like an eternity had passed since I had first looked into her bedroom that morning and my nightmare began. I quickly looked away.

To the right of her bedroom door was a linen closet, and the door next to that was my bedroom. Before entering, I turned to face the living room. Although the distance between my mother and me was only about twelve feet, fear gripped me. As I walked into my bedroom, I felt cut off from the rest of the house. It was the first time that I realized that I could not be alone without feeling anxious. Hurriedly, I went to my dresser drawer and pulled out the items that I needed.

Walking back into the living room, I noticed that Officer Strubel had returned. He and my mom were talking quietly. I remember staring blankly out of a small window to the right of them, finding it difficult to focus on what they were saying. This mental confusion was something that would plague me for many weeks after the assault. Gradually, I became aware that they were discussing the severed phone line. Officer Struble was informing my mom that the phone company had been called. He expected them to arrive at my house within the next hour to repair the line. My thoughts flashed back to earlier that morning. I remembered hearing the unnerving silence on the phone instead of the dial tone after the intruder had left my home.

It was after ten thirty when we walked out onto the porch and I was finally able to talk to Joanne. "Are you alright, Jules?" she asked, as she cautiously approached me. Putting her arms around me, she hugged me tightly.

My voice quivered when I spoke. "I'll be okay, Joanne," I said unconvincingly. "My mom is taking me to the hospital for some tests." Then I added, "I'm sorry, Joanne. He was in your room." I was unaware of what the police had told her exactly, but I wanted to prepare her for the mess she would see when she entered her room. Without her permission, the

26

rapist, and then the police, had gone through her personal belongings. Surely she would feel as though she had also been violated.

The drive to the hospital took about fifteen minutes. In the car, the conversation with my mother was brief. She asked me if I was sure about my decision to have the rape kit done. My response did not waiver. I was determined to do whatever was needed to help convict the man who had assaulted me.

We arrived at the emergency room a few minutes after eleven a.m. My mother addressed the woman behind the desk. "My daughter was raped," she said, quietly, so that she would not attract the attention of the people sitting nearby.

SIX

Rape Kit

Even though my mother had spoken softly, in my mind, each person in the waiting room was staring right at me and knew what had happened. After signing the required hospital forms, I was asked to have a seat in the waiting room. My stomach felt queasy. *Can't they put me in a back room somewhere?* Tears welled up in my eyes. The thought of sitting in that waiting room with all of those people watching me cry was unbearable. With my head down, I followed my mother to two empty chairs. Slowly, I sat down, unable to look at anyone near me.

As I waited in that emergency room, clutching my bag of clothes, I was suddenly conscious of my physical appearance. My purple sweatshirt and pants were the ones that I had worn to sleep the night before. It was the same outfit that I was wearing when the rapist attacked me. I had not had a shower, brushed my teeth, or combed my hair. I had not even emptied my bladder yet. I made the effort to smooth my shoulder-length hair with my fingers. Reaching down around my chair, I was able to find my purse. Locating a small compact, I opened it and looked at myself in the mirror. The face that looked back at me was both startling and unfamiliar. Her eyes were red and swollen. There was a long, thin scratch on her right cheek. Her skin was pale, and there was a look of despair on her face. Finding a tissue, I wiped the tears from under my eyes. In a side pocket of my purse I searched for and found my eyeliner. In a desperate attempt to look normal, I steadied my hand just long enough to outline my eyes.

Several years later, Joanne would tell me that my face changed on that day. When viewing a photograph of me, she could tell whether it was taken before or after the assault. She explained that there was something missing in my smile and my laugh that she had known since we were children. Hearing Joanne say this didn't surprise me; I felt that my passion for life had been lost, or was buried deep within me. My eyes had lost their sparkle.

I spent the remainder of the time in the emergency room fighting back my tears. It was draining trying to hide my shabby appearance and inner turmoil. Losing control of my emotions in public made me feel weak and vulnerable. In my mind, it was important to appear strong and uninjured.

My mother and I waited in that emergency room for an excruciating hour and fifteen minutes. It is one of the most painful memories I have of that day. Finally, I heard my name being called from a doorway behind my chair. The time was now twelve thirty p.m.—lunch time, but I did not think of food. A petite nurse led my mother and me into an exam room. She introduced herself as Susan and apologized for the long wait. Her kindness helped to ease some of the tension that I was feeling. After verifying the information on the hospital form, she asked my mother to wait outside of the room. I was grateful that my mom would not be in the room for the exam. It seemed senseless to expose her to any more trauma of the assault.

Susan pulled out a white box from an overhead cabinet. She acted very professional; however, she seemed unacquainted with this particular rape kit. I remember her reading the directions as though she had not seen them before. This made me somewhat anxious, but still I felt comfortable in her care. Finally, she turned in my direction and laid a large white cloth down on the floor in front of the table. After handing me a hospital gown, she instructed me to stand on the white cloth while removing my clothes. My purple sweats should be left in the center of the cloth, hopefully trapping any hairs or fibers that might have been left behind by the rapist. Then I was to put on the hospital gown and sit on the exam table.

Susan left the room to give me privacy. I did as she asked, grateful to finally rid myself of the soiled clothes. When I sat on the table, I noticed for the first time that there were several large red scrapes on each of my wrists. Memories of my hands being tied behind my back returned. Quickly, I looked toward the door, hoping the nurse would interrupt my thoughts before I began to relive the rest of that awful morning.

A few minutes later, she returned and neatly folded up the white cloth, enclosing my clothes. Then she put the entire pile of fabric into a plastic bag and labeled it.

With clipboard in hand, Susan asked me a few general questions about my health, then asked me to explain what had happened that morning. In order to know where to look for evidence, the medical authorities needed to know the specifics of the rape. Not expecting this question from her, tears again welled up in my eyes. As I tried to compose myself, Susan reached over to me and put her hand on top of mine. I could clearly feel the concern and tenderness of this woman almost as if it flowed from her hand into mine. Instantly my thoughts flashed back to Officer Struble. Within each of them, I sensed a kind and loving spirit that was able to break through my suffering.

Never losing her soft expression, she listened and took notes as I described the rape for the third time that morning. When I finished, she put her clipboard down on a nearby table. "Normally we'd ask for a urine specimen to do a pregnancy test, but since you have your period, that won't be necessary. Can you wait to use the bathroom until after the exam?" I nodded my head. I was numb to any urge that I had to urinate.

The next step was to trim the tips of my fingernails in the event I had scratched the assailant. I held out my hands so she could cut what she needed, although I was doubtful that I had been able to scratch him. She put my nail clippings in a small bag and labeled it. Then she combed through the hair on my head, being careful to catch any hairs that fell out in the process. They would be looking for any stray hairs that the rapist might have lost during the assault. Once again, I doubted that this would be of help since the rapist was wearing a stocking over his head the entire time he was with me. The nurse explained that the rape kit also required her to pull about ten hairs from my head as part of the evidence. It was important that these hairs be pulled, and not cut, in order to obtain the roots. *If this is what the authorities need to convict my assailant, then they can have it.*

Susan hesitated before explaining the next step. She needed to comb through my pubic hair with a special comb, collecting all stray hairs, and pull about ten hairs from this area of my body. Lying down on the table, I closed my eyes while she collected the evidence she needed. Her peaceful demeanor helped me endure the trauma of the rape kit.

Finally, she lined up the plastic bags of evidence on a tray, then explained that more samples would be taken by the doctor who would do the pelvic exam. While we waited for the doctor, she explained that he would be taking both vaginal and rectal swabs in an effort to find samples of the rapist's semen. He would also be collecting samples to test for any sexually transmitted diseases. This exam would only check for diseases present before the rape. It was too early to tell if I had been infected during the rape. This thought had not occurred to me during the hectic pace of the morning. *What if the rapist has AIDS? Could I still die as a result of the rape?* The perpetrator did not wear a condom. Suddenly it felt as though a ticking bomb was inside of me, ready to explode at any moment.

Susan told me it would take at least six months for me to test positive for the AIDS virus if I had been infected by the rapist. She said that whether or not I would be tested for this disease during the following year was my own choice.

Twenty agonizing minutes passed until the doctor appeared. He seemed rushed and somewhat annoyed. As I lay on the table during the examination, he became the fourth person to ask me to explain what had happened during the rape. By now it felt like I was reading a script. The tears and emotion had disappeared.

The pelvic exam was unusually painful. Maybe it was due to the trauma of the rape or possibly my inability to relax, but I remember wishing that he would slow down and work gently. Thankfully, Susan held my hand through much of the exam.

When the doctor finished, he walked out of the room abruptly, leaving me feeling as though I had done something wrong. This was the second time that morning that I had experienced this type of response. Detective

Shanahan had also been distant and insensitive. It was becoming apparent that I would encounter both negative and positive reactions from others as a result of reporting this crime.

The trauma of the emergency room was finally over. I was free to use the bathroom and get dressed. Wearing a fresh set of clothes, I walked with my mom out of the hospital to the car. *Finally I can take a shower!* Sitting in the passenger seat, I remember staring out the side window of the car, too preoccupied to notice the scenery.

Suddenly I wasn't sure if home was where I wanted to go. *Will just walking into my house bring back the nightmare?*

SEVEN

My Home, a Crime Scene

Home. The place where I took refuge after a long, hard day of working and studying. The place where I found peace and security. Now, as we approached my block, I could see the front and side yards of my house from the corner. The police cars were gone, and Joanne's car was missing from the driveway. I would walk into an empty house. Mom drove up to the front of my house and parked. I was in a hurry to get in the shower, but afraid of going inside my house. Walking slowly up my front walkway, I looked at the yard. The perpetrator, the police had told me, had moved one of the chairs from the front of my house to the rear window that he had climbed through. Now, I saw that someone had put it back where it belonged on the porch.

Unlocking my front door, I nervously stepped inside. My mother followed. A cold chill permeated my body. Standing there, I realized that my safe and cozy haven was now a crime scene. A pervading atmosphere of terror hung in the air. A rush of anxiety overcame me, and I was unable to move. With the exception of the bathroom and laundry room, I could see into each room of my house from the front door. All of the stuffed animals that had littered the hallway had been put back on Joanne's bed. A stereo speaker that had been knocked over during the rape had been put back in its place. Yet, my living room seemed different somehow. Its warmth had been replaced with an icy, threatening stillness.

A sudden knock at the front door startled me. Turning around, I saw

George on my front porch. Opening the screen door, I invited him in. The look of concern I had seen on his face that morning still lingered. He wanted to let us know that the phone company had been to my house and reconnected the phone line. I walked over to the phone, picked up the receiver, and was relieved to hear the dial tone. George continued talking to my mom. Eager for my shower, I excused myself and left the room.

Closing the bathroom door was uncomfortable. The idea of being alone, even with my mom in the next room, bothered me. Reaching into the bathtub, I turned on the faucet and waited for the water to heat up. *Maybe if I take a shower in really hot water, I will finally feel clean.* I waited until the water was so hot, I could just barely tolerate it. The bathroom filled with steam, but fear prevented me from opening the outside window to let it escape.

Scrubbing every inch of my body, I attempted to remove all traces of the rapist. *This is going to be an impossible task.* I washed my hair three times. Twenty minutes later, I ran out of hot water and was forced to turn the shower off. I felt only slightly cleaner. The fresh set of clothes I had put on at the hospital seemed dirty now because they had touched my un-showered body. Reaching for my bathrobe, I left those clothes hanging on the back of the bathroom door.

After brushing my teeth, I cracked open the bathroom door. When I didn't hear George's voice, I walked across the hallway and into my bedroom. Finding another clean outfit, I put it on.

It was two o'clock. I felt like Friday was already a week long, and I was beginning to think it would never end. Joanne wouldn't be coming home until Monday, when her parents returned. I felt it would be impossible to be alone in the house for even one minute, let alone three days! I decided to stay with my parents until Joanne came home. Possibly, when I returned home on Monday, everything would be back to normal and I would once again feel comfortable and safe in my precious home. After locating a small suitcase in a closet upstairs, I packed enough clothes to wear during the long weekend.

Before leaving, I locked all of my windows and filled the food bowl for Joanne's cat, Brandy. I would call Joanne later so she would know to check on her during the next few days. As I pulled the front door closed, I double-checked to make sure it was also locked. Still facing my house, I heard my name being called from behind me. Turning my head, I saw Barb, another neighbor, approaching me. Closing my screen door, I walked to meet her. She wanted to let me know that she had spoken to one of the police officers that morning. She said that my neighbors were all aware of what had happened to me, and they wanted me to know that they were available to help me if I needed anything. She also wanted me to know that she told the police that I was a "good girl," didn't throw wild parties, and didn't have strange men spend the night.

What does any of that have to do with being raped? Is she saying that it's usually the "bad girls" who are sexually assaulted? I realized for the first time that many people believe that victims of rape have done something to provoke their attack.

My parents lived in the city of Warren, about six miles from my home. Still feeling dazed, I was uncomfortable driving my own car, so once again, I rode with Mom. I was feeling helpless. It had been five years since I had moved out of my parents' house. I had worked hard for my independence. Now I had lost it all.

The anger that I felt toward the man who assaulted me was growing. My fears were also multiplying. *Will the police be able to find him?* Knowing he was still on the streets terrified me. Until he was caught, I would feel like he was watching me, waiting for me to be alone again. *He knows who I am and where I live, but I have no idea who he is.* Because I saw him walk past my kitchen window when he left my house, I believed I might recognize him, but it was such a brief moment. If he altered his appearance, I might not be able to distinguish him from other men with similar features. His physical reign of terror had ended that morning, but the psychological horror was just beginning.

EIGHT

In the Arms of My Family

As we pulled into my parents' driveway, my dad approached the car, still dressed in his work clothes. The look of grief in his eyes told me that he knew what had happened. *Who told him?* Dad worked as a pipe fitter on a construction site. While he was working, it was difficult to contact him by phone. My mom had been with me all day, and I knew she had not talked with him. When I opened the car door, my dad was standing directly in front of me, his arms outstretched. Safe in my father's embrace, I relaxed, and was unable to hold back my tears.

"We love you," was all that he said. For that brief moment, I felt safe. As we walked toward the front door, I asked my dad who had told him about the break-in.

"Your friend Nancy," he answered. Apparently, Joanne had called this close friend of mine earlier in the day, and Nancy had called my parents' house to ask how I was doing. At the time, my father had no idea what she was talking about. Unfortunately, my friend was put in the dreadful position of telling him all that she knew.

In my parents' house, I sat down on their couch and turned on the television. Maybe it would take my mind off of what had happened. By now, it was about four p.m. Eight hours had passed since the man with the stocking-covered face jumped from Joanne's closet. It was an image I could not erase from my memory. Over and over again, I replayed this scene in my mind, making it impossible to concentrate on the television show I was watching.

Realizing that I had not eaten since the day before, Mom began to prepare dinner. Food still didn't interest me. As she tore apart the lettuce for the salad, I didn't even think to help her. Mom then reminded me that our family reunion was to take place on Saturday.

"Tomorrow?" I asked.

"Yes," Mom responded. "You can come with Dad and me."

I had forgotten all about the family reunion! This seemed more than I could handle. *How can I break through this mental fog and carry on a conversation? Will my attendance make everyone uncomfortable? If my parents decide to go without me, will I be able to stay here by myself?* The thought of being alone, even at the house I grew up in, terrified me.

My memory of that evening with my parents is a blur. Vaguely, I remember nibbling at my dinner and saying very little. We talked about what we would do to provide additional security for my home. I recalled the conversation that I had with my dad about guns less than two weeks earlier. Although I had believed that I could never use a gun on an intruder, I realized I had been wrong. Instinctively I would do whatever was needed in order to survive. Sometimes doing nothing is what feels right in order to stay alive.

Lying awake in my parents' guest room, unable to fall asleep, is what I remember most about that grueling night. The thought of nightmares invading my dreams kept me from closing my eyes. Home invasions and rapes were things that happened to other people. In the secure world that I grew up in, family and friends never got hurt. *If something this terrible can happen to me, now anything is possible.* I felt like a walking target for all predators. They could be lurking around every corner. I also believed that God either couldn't or wouldn't stop these tragedies from happening to me. I no longer understood the purpose of prayers. Since I had felt God's presence during the rape, I could not deny His existence. He provided me comfort, but He still allowed the intruder to hurt me. I was unable to reconcile these contradictory thoughts. Somehow I believed that I should be angry with God, but emotionally I didn't feel it. Now I would not only have to sort out how I felt about the rape, but also how I perceived God.

I kept looking at the closed bedroom window, preferring the stuffy heat rather than exposing myself to the dangers of the night. Lying there, I decided to attend our family reunion. It would be more comfortable than staying alone. My parents had called my grandmother, so my family knew about the rape. I sensed that my dad's family would not be afraid to bring it up. That would be okay. Talking about it would be better than pretending it didn't happen. The last time I looked at the clock, it read three a.m. Fortunately, I would not remember my dreams that night.

The following morning, not wanting to disturb me, my parents moved quietly around the house. When I finally woke up, it was almost eleven. Maneuvering my way out of bed, I noticed that every muscle in my body ached. *Is this soreness a result of the struggle from yesterday?* Searching for aspirin in the medicine cabinet, I was in a hurry to get rid of the pain. It was a grim reminder of the assault.

It was an hour's drive to the farm where our family gathering was taking place. The property was the home of my uncle, one of my dad's younger brothers. As we drove up the long, gravel driveway, I was able to see about twenty family members sitting at tables that had been set up on the lawn. As Dad parked the car, I became more apprehensive. Mom handed me a dish to carry, and I was grateful to have something to do.

Avoiding any eye contact with my relatives, I walked directly toward the side door of the house. As I climbed the stairs that led to the kitchen, I noticed my dad's youngest brother standing nearby. Without hesitating, he reached out to hug me. The expression on his face was one of compassion and sorrow. His welcoming embrace made me feel safe and loved. Releasing his hug, he looked directly at me. The expression on his face had changed from concern to anger. "I'd like to kill that bastard!" he said, through gritted teeth. His reaction was one that I would see over and over again in the coming weeks. Right then, anger felt good to me. In a way, it was a distraction from the fear. Apparently, it was an emotional release for my family also.

While visiting my family at the farm that day, I received many warm and consoling hugs. Memories of their love and support would help lift my spirits during some of the more difficult days ahead.

It was about nine p.m. when we returned to my parents' home. After closing the windows, I collapsed onto the bed. It was even warmer than the previous evening, but I didn't care. Thankfully, the nightmares left me alone for one more night, but I would have to face my worst nightmare on Monday. I would have to go home.

NINE

Afraid in My Own Home

Still no answer! Frustrated, I hung up the phone. I was at my parents' house. It was Monday evening, and I was anxious to return to my beloved bungalow. However, if Joanne wasn't there, I was going to wait until she was. Convinced that the rapist was still watching my house, I was sure that he would return the minute I was left alone. My renewed dependence upon my parents and Joanne made me feel like a child.

It was about seven p.m. when Joanne finally answered the phone. Pretending as though I was calling for the first time, I told her that I was on my way home. My mother drove me.

In the car, I thought about the one person I needed to call and talk to about the assault. For three days, I had been avoiding a phone call to Gary. It would be extremely difficult to say the words, "I was raped." Until now, I had only said them to Officer Strubel and on the phone to Lisa, immediately following the assault. I needed Gary now more than ever, but I was worried about how he would react to hearing about the rape.

Turning the corner, onto my tree-lined street, I could see Joanne's car parked in the driveway and I felt better. My car was there, too, right where I had parked it the night before the rape. It seemed like so long ago. *I wish I was still that fearless young woman that stumbled wearily into her house after a long day at work.*

As Mom's car approached my house, I couldn't help but think back to how different my life would be if I would have paid more attention to the warning signs. *Would a light in my backyard have prevented the assault? What if I had locked all of the windows and doors in my house that night? Maybe I should have allowed my family to continue staying with me at night the whole time Joanne was gone.* It must have been obvious to the intruder that I was the only one home when he saw just one car parked in the driveway. I did not have the answers to these questions, so I refused to let them upset me further.

As we pulled up to the house, I saw Sean's car parked at the curb. The front door of the house was closed, and the light in the living room was on. Although I had been anxious to get home, I was suddenly leery about staying there. Grabbing my overnight bag, I looked at my mom as if I was leaving for war. As I hugged her, I saw fear in her eyes. Although I didn't realize it then, she probably had a more difficult time watching me disappear into my house than I had walking into it.

Sean and Joanne were both sitting on the couch in the living room. Before the rape, it was the room that I felt most relaxed in. *Will I ever feel that way again?*

Joanne greeted me with her usual "Hi Jules." The words were the same as always, but her normally, playful attitude was missing. Then there was silence. It seemed difficult for either of us to think of what to say next. Carefully locking the door behind me, I barricaded us in the house. Instinctively, I scanned the house for any open windows. Putting my purse and my suitcase on the floor, I sat down on the wooden rocking chair that faced the couch. Staring at Joanne and Sean for several moments, I finally spoke. "It's okay to talk about it. Actually, I would like to talk about it," I said.

Joanne and Sean spent the next couple of hours letting me talk and listening to my concerns. Discussing my fears seemed to lesson their intensity. I learned that Joanne was deeply affected by what had happened. It was through her bedroom window that the rapist had entered. He had rummaged through her dresser drawers, taken her stuffed animals, and hid in her closet. The cord that the rapist used to tie my hands behind my back had been cut from her fan. The personal violation that she experienced would forever be etched into Joanne's memory and would affect her sense of security.

Glancing at the time, I noticed it was after nine thirty. If I was going to call Gary tonight, I needed to do it soon. My hands were trembling as I picked up the phone and stretched the cord into my bedroom. Sitting on the floor, leaning against my bed, I began dialing. After pressing the first few buttons, I quickly hung up. *What will I say first? Why am I afraid?* I thought about how much I missed him, picked up the phone again, and dialed his number. Gary had a great sense of humor and he made me laugh. Talking to him always lifted my spirits. Nervously I waited. The phone rang three times, but there was no answer. A part of me breathed a sigh of relief. After the fourth ring, I heard a familiar "Hello."

"Hi Gary. It's Julie."

"How are you, kiddo?"

Not knowing what to say next, I asked him how his week had been. Although he went through a detailed account of his work week, I was unable to focus on a single word he was saying.

"Julie?" I heard him ask. "Are you still there?"

"Yes, I'm here," I responded quietly.

"Is there something wrong?" Apparently I had not responded to something he had said.

"Gary, my house was broken into on Friday morning."

There was silence on the other end of the line. He seemed to be waiting for more information. I continued talking.

"I was home when it happened." Even I could hear the quiver in my voice.

Still he said nothing. His prolonged silence wasn't helping.

"He was a rapist," I blurted out. It was a relief to have finally told him, but his unresponsiveness was scaring me. "Are you still there?" I asked him nervously.

"Yes, I'm here," he responded in an unemotional tone.

"Why aren't you saying anything, Gary?" I was close to tears.

"I don't know what to say, Julie. I'm sorry that happened to you." He was speaking quickly now, as he always did when he was nervous.

What did I expect him to say? There were no words that would make everything all right. I wanted to see his face, but he was thousands of miles

45

away. I hoped he would come home to be with me. He didn't offer. I didn't ask.

"Are you hurt?" Gary finally asked.

Not sure what he meant by this question, I simply answered "I'm okay." During the days following the rape, I was often asked that same question. Once people learned that the rapist had not bruised or cut my body, it seemed to comfort them. It appeared that they didn't understand the injuries I sustained went beyond my physical body.

Briefly, I told Gary how the rapist had broken into our house through Joanne's bedroom window while I was home alone. He listened quietly and asked few questions. Believing that he needed some time to think about what he had heard, I told him that I was tired and wanted to go to bed.

"I'll call you soon, Julie," Gary replied.

"All right Gary," I responded sadly.

After hanging up, a feeling of abandonment swept through me. I had been hoping that Gary would console me, but the conversation left me feeling empty. The last time we spoke, he told me that he loved me. *Has he met someone else since then?* I couldn't believe that he suddenly no longer cared about me. Feeling hopeless, alone, and exhausted, I sat there in a long silence, before lashing out at God. *What have I done to deserve this? This is more than I can handle! I'd be better off if the monster had killed me.* The security of my home and my autonomy were the things I valued above all else in my life, and they had both been ripped away from me. I blamed God for my misfortune. He could have stopped this rape and He didn't. He was allowing me to suffer.

The sound of Sean's voice pulled me out of my silence. He was getting ready to leave. I took the phone back into the living room. "Sean, you can't go!" I pleaded. "Can you stay here tonight?"

"Of course I'm staying. I'm just running home to get a change of clothes. Will you be okay until I get back?" he asked.

"Just hurry!" we said in unison.

"Lock the door behind me," were the last words Sean said as he pulled it shut. My hands were reaching for the doorknob before the words even left his mouth.

This was a moment I had dreaded. Joanne and I were alone in the house, not knowing whether the rapist was sitting outside somewhere, still watching us. Moving into the kitchen, I closed the blinds on both windows. We sat at the kitchen table, as we had so many times before. Usually we talked about work, complaining about our bosses or what was said around the water cooler. Tonight we talked about how we could feel safe again. Better locks on the windows were first on the agenda. An alarm system would help me feel less vulnerable, but that was something I couldn't afford. My dad had already bought a large, bright light that he was planning to install in my backyard.

Although my conversation with Gary was still in my thoughts, the hurt was too deep to discuss it with Joanne that night. Maybe he would call me tomorrow after having some time to think about what I had told him. Clinging to that thought gave me hope that tomorrow could be a better day.

The time was approaching eleven p.m. when Sean came back with his clothes. Although I wasn't looking forward to the solitude of my bedroom, I knew I should try and get a good night's sleep. My shift at work began at eight o'clock in the morning, and my boss was expecting me. Although I knew that they would understand if I asked for a few days off, I was in a hurry for my life to return to normal. Not taking any time off made me feel as though I had won a small battle. If I stayed home, it meant the rapist had won. Thankfully, the three-day weekend had given me an extra day to recover.

After saying goodnight to Joanne and Sean, I checked the locks on each of the windows in the kitchen and the living room. Stopping in the bathroom to brush my teeth and take out my contacts, I checked that window also. Then I checked each window in the house a second time.

As I pulled down my bedspread, I dreaded going to sleep. I turned off the light and climbed in bed, wearing my glasses so I could see the door and window clearly. I tried to fill my thoughts with pleasant memories, so I could avoid the nightmares. An hour later, my eyes were still wide open. They kept darting from the door to the window and back again, afraid that either might burst open at any moment. It's possible that I would have felt safer sleeping in a dark alley. When I finally slept, the nightmares were even worse than I had expected. In each one, I was chased by a dark figure without a face. Who it was, or where we were, was a blur, yet I instinctively knew that if I didn't keep running, I would die.

TEN

Triple Jeopardy: My Life, My Job, My Home

When my alarm went off on Tuesday, I was exhausted, but alive. I was grateful to see the morning light seeping into my room from the edges of the window shade. Still wearing my glasses, I got out of bed and peered out my bedroom door into the hallway. Quietly, I tiptoed into the living room, determined to open the mini-blinds to let in the sunlight so I could see clearly as I walked through each room of my house. Moving from the living room to the kitchen, I was startled by a slight movement that I saw out of the corner of my eye. Turning my head, I saw Joanne's cat walking slowly out of her bedroom. Brandy was looking for her breakfast and began following me.

Certain that no one was hiding in our kitchen, I headed back toward the bathroom. The door leading to the dormer that occupied the second floor of my bungalow caught my attention. Slowly, I opened the door and looked up the steep, narrow stairway that led to the second-floor room. If I could summon the courage to get to the top of the stairs, I would be able to see the entire room with one quick glance and know that no one was hiding there. Holding my breath, I began the ascent. At the top of the stairs, I braced myself for the worst and peered around the corner. It was empty! As I looked around at the plain white walls and slanted ceiling, I felt the tension leave my body.

I hurried through my morning routine. Joanne and Sean were just getting up as I finished taking a shower and was heading back to my room.

"Morning, Joanne," I said, pulling the towel off my wet hair.

"Good morning," she replied, finishing her yawn.

"How did you sleep?" I asked her.

"With one eye open," she responded wearily.

"Are you stopping anywhere after work today?"

"No, I don't think so," she responded, as she brushed her wavy brown hair out of her eyes.

"I'm worried about coming home to an empty house, Joanne," I confessed, feeling like an immature twelve-year-old.

Joanne nodded, understandingly. "Don't worry. I'll make sure that I come straight home." She went into the bathroom and closed the door.

In less than twenty minutes I had finished dressing, grabbed a quick piece of toast for breakfast, and was on my way out the front door. Once outside, I was keenly aware of my surroundings. Surveying the street for any unfamiliar cars or strange, dark-haired men, I left my porch and dashed towards the driveway. Holding my keys, I felt my heart pounding as I struggled to unlock my car door. The rapist had watched me without my knowing it before the attack. Now I believed that he could still be hiding behind a neighbor's bush or sitting in his car somewhere. *Will this horrendous fear go away when he is caught? What if he is never found?*

It seemed like it took forever to get my car unlocked. Once the door opened, I lowered myself into the driver's seat, slammed the door shut, and quickly relocked it. For a brief moment, I felt safe. Taking a deep breath and letting it out slowly I thought, *My fears are irrational. There is no way that monster will take the chance of being seen around my house this soon.* Still, the intense fear did not leave me. Pulling out of my neighborhood, I turned on the radio in an attempt to get my mind off the rape. Yet, the image of the monster leaping from the closet and pushing me to the floor continued to plague me. Then my thoughts turned to my coworkers, with whom I had worked for less than a year. *Do they all know what happened to me? Should I talk about it? How will I focus on work when it seems impossible to put the rape out of my mind?* Fortunately, Lisa would also be working the day shift that day. She was the coworker and friend who had answered the phone when I called into work the morning of the rape. It was reassuring to know that there would be at least one person I could confide in.

As I pulled into the multi-story parking garage next to the Renaissance Center in downtown Detroit, it occurred to me that I remembered almost nothing about my drive to work. This memory lapse terrified me. *Will I be able to react in time if faced with a dangerous situation on the road? Maybe I shouldn't have come back to work so early.* It was almost as if I had closed my eyes during the forty-minute drive in rush-hour traffic. Suddenly, the thought came to me that I was not alone on that trip to work. It was as though someone else had taken control of the steering wheel and guided me safely to my destination. *Is God protecting me from further danger?*

"Thank you," I whispered, as I pulled into a parking space. *Is this truly another appearance by God in my life? Why has it taken me twenty-six years to recognize His intervention?*

As soon as I stepped out of the car, I again felt vulnerable and unsafe in the parking garage. I was exposed to all of the dangerous criminals that I believed were hiding around every corner. Hurrying into the office building, I was anxious to get to the twelfth floor where employees with keys were the only ones who could enter. Stepping into the elevator, I studied every male face in that small space.

Working downtown was something I had grown to enjoy. The views from our upper-floor computer room were beautiful, especially during the early-morning hours, when one could look out over the river to Windsor, Ontario as the brilliant colors from the sunrise were painted onto the sky. When the elevator stopped and the doors opened, I stepped out into a small lobby and used my key to open the door that led to the computer room where I worked. About twenty-five people worked on this floor during the day and I knew I would be facing some of them when I entered the room. Several people on midnights would also be finishing up their work during the first half hour of my shift. Since the training program that I had just finished had been at a different location, two weeks had

51

passed since I had spoken to any of them. Nervously, I opened the door a crack and peered into the room where a large printer was located. One of my coworkers, Paul, was unloading a stack of paper from the back of the printer. With great hesitancy, I stepped into the room.

"Good morning, Julie!" Paul said with enthusiasm. "How were your classes?" His cheerful reaction to my entrance suggested that he had not heard about the assault. Forcing a smile, I looked toward Paul, but avoided his eyes.

"I'm glad it's over!" I replied. "It was a long and exhausting two weeks, but I survived."

"You look tired," he responded, as I walked past the printer toward the room that housed the large, main computer. Through the small, rectangular windows on the doors, I was able to see the night-shift supervisor talking to David, the man who supervised the day-shift crew. Opening the door, I felt the rush of cold air that normally flowed through this room. The loud hum of the many electronic devices prevented me from hearing what the supervisors were saying, but I knew they were discussing the jobs that had not been finished during the night. Saying nothing, I walked up and stood behind them. Determined to focus on today's workload, I listened to their conversation.

When David noticed that I was standing behind him, he smiled and acknowledged my presence. "Hey, Julie! Glad to have you back. How was the training?"

"It was the longest two weeks of my life," I responded. As I had done with Paul, I avoided looking directly into David's eyes. Already, I was beginning to understand that rape is a subject that is not talked about openly. If my coworkers didn't know what happened or didn't want to talk about it, I wouldn't either.

"Do you mind if I go to say hello to Lisa before I start working?" I asked David.

"Go ahead. Take your time."

Leaving the computer room, I hoped that I would not bump into anyone else on the way to Lisa's desk. Quietly walking through the hallway where the offices were located, I spotted Lisa's long, blond hair through the doorway in the office at the end of the corridor. Without saying a word, I slipped into the empty chair next to her desk. Sensing my presence, she looked up, and her eyes widened. "Julie, you're back!" she shrieked. "I'm so glad to see you!" She stood up, leaned over my chair, and hugged me.

"Thanks, Lisa. Knowing that you would be here made it easier for me to come in to work today."

"Are you okay?" Lisa asked in a hushed tone. Each time I was asked that question I was unsure of how I should respond. I was not okay! Physically, I appeared normal and unharmed. Emotionally, I was a wreck, although I sometimes sensed that my family and friends did not want to hear that. Uncomfortable describing the full extent of my "injuries," I simply told Lisa that I was struggling. At least in front of her, I didn't have to pretend that nothing had happened.

"Who knows about the rape, Lisa?" I finally asked her.

"Jeff is the only person I told." Jeff was the manager of computer operations. It was now clear that he hadn't shared this information with anyone.

"Thanks for listening, Lisa. I better get to work. Will I see you at lunchtime?"

"Definitely. Take care, Julie."

For the next few hours, I struggled to get my work done. Shortly before lunch, Jeff called me into his office. Apparently it had taken him all morning to develop enough courage to talk to me. Through the large windows behind him, I was able to look out over the waterfront of the Detroit River. Normally, I would have admired the view of the sun reflecting off the water, but today I was focused on the somber expression on my manager's face.

"Have a seat." Jeff motioned for me to sit down. In the past, he would have just pulled me aside in the computer room if he had something to say to me. He then sat down on the opposite side of his desk and nervously shuffled the papers in front of him until he had cleared his entire desk. The silence while he did this was awkward. Finally he said, "If there's anything we can do for you, Julie, don't hesitate to ask. If you need to take some time off, I understand." His eyes shifted back and forth between my eyes and his empty desk.

"Thank you, but I would rather come to work than stay at home," I responded, with no further explanation.

Jeff continued. "Normally when an employee returns from their operations training, they are given a test based on the information learned during the previous two weeks. Usually this test is given shortly after you return from your classes, but in your case I will let you postpone it, if that will be easier for you."

It was common knowledge that employees who failed this test were asked to leave the company. Several employees that I knew of had lost their jobs for this reason. If I delayed taking the test, my memory of the training would not be as sharp. Yet if I took the test this week, I didn't think I would be able to focus long enough to study for it. It was a struggle to even remember that it was Tuesday. In addition to the stress that I was already feeling, if I failed this test, I could lose my job and my home. Regardless of the outcome, I wanted to get the test over with. "I want to take it as soon as possible," I said with determination.

He told me that Friday would be the day. Exactly one week after the rape—I had only three days to review my notes from the courses I had attended.

"I'm sorry, Julie," Jeff said quietly as I stood up to leave the room. His concern appeared genuine. Unable to think of a verbal response, I nodded my head.

As I left Jeff's office, I felt as if my world was crumbling around me. *How can I possibly concentrate on studying for this test?* Because of the rape, I had missed the final day of training. I was so traumatized by the assault that everything I learned during those two weeks seemed blocked from my memory. My mind wasn't functioning normally, and I didn't know how to fix it. *How can I think clearly or rationally as long as I am in this constant state of worry that someone is watching me, and that my life is in danger every second of the day?*

Wanting to avoid my coworkers, I headed directly to the women's restroom. Entering, I looked around to make sure I was alone. Directly in front of me was a large mirror above the sinks. I turned my head to avoid seeing my pale skin, dark circles under my eyes, and troubled expression.

Refusing to see these changes allowed me to hold on to the belief that one day I would wake up and my life would be back to normal.

Throughout the remainder of that day, I worked in constant worry of making mistakes and performed my responsibilities slowly. I would find out later that my coworkers sensed that something was wrong, but didn't feel comfortable asking me questions.

Because those of us who worked in the operations department were required to change shifts every three months, there were only a handful of fellow employees that I felt close to. One of these was Richard, the second-shift supervisor—a large, handsome man in his mid-thirties, with a great sense of humor. He was easy to work for—an honest man who spoke his mind and offered encouragement to each new employee. I only saw him for the thirty minutes a day that our shifts overlapped between four and four thirty p.m., yet he noticed that I was "different," and asked if anything was wrong. It was clear that he was unaware of the rape. Apparently, Jeff was the only manager who knew about the attack and he wasn't talking about it. The crime of rape was taboo—it carried an aura of shame, humiliation, and secrecy. I told Richard what had happened. He listened intently and did not hesitate to ask me for additional information. It was comforting to find someone who was not afraid to talk to me. Richard offered many words of advice during the first few days after the rape. Among his ideas was that I should purchase a gun and keep it near me as I slept. If the rapist decided to pay another visit to my house, I would be ready for him. Although I was desperate for some protection at home, I knew that I did not want to keep a gun in my house. My fear was that my heightened sensitivity to strange noises would cause me to accidentally shoot Joanne or Sean.

During my lunch breaks that first week, I studied the notes from my training in an attempt to prepare myself for the test. One day, I stayed after work to study, feeling safer in my work environment than at home in Royal Oak. Every night that week, before leaving work, I called home to make sure Joanne, Sean, or my Dad was there.

During that first week, my parents and I did everything that we could to create a more secure atmosphere in my home. My dad installed a light in my backyard that turned on automatically at dusk. The police department had suggested installing a specific type of lock on each window, making them impossible to open without breaking the glass. We purchased and installed the locks they had recommended. To relieve me from the task of checking each closet whenever I returned home, we put chain locks on each of these doors. We also put a lock on the door leading to the second floor. If I walked into the house and all the chains were secure, I knew it was impossible for someone to be hiding behind those closed doors.

We also bought an intercom system to allow me to communicate with my next-door neighbor, George, at the touch of a button. All of these items provided me only slight relief from my constant fear.

Every spare moment that week I spent looking at my notes from work and trying to study. Although I was able to understand the words when I read them, it seemed impossible for me to retain the information five minutes later. Nightmares continued to interrupt my sleep, and each morning I woke up exhausted. Friday morning, I was a nervous wreck when I went to work. I was going to fail the test. I was going to lose everything I had worked for: my job, my income, my home.

ELEVEN

A Defining Moment

At work, in a final, desperate attempt to learn my notes, I decided to study them on my lunch hour and take the test in the afternoon. When I looked at my notes, it was as if I was reading them for the first time.

At the end of my lunch hour I knew that I couldn't put it off any longer. Hesitantly, I walked down the hall to Lisa's cubicle. As training coordinator, she would give me the test. "Are you ready?" she asked, looking up at me.

"I just want to get it over with," I mumbled.

She led me to a small room, where she placed the test booklet on a desk.

"I'm scared, Lisa," I confided.

"You'll do fine. I have confidence in you." Then she looked directly into my eyes and whispered, "Good luck, Julie." She left, closing the door behind her.

For several minutes I stared at the cover of the test booklet, then, with great reluctance, I opened it to the first page of questions. There was no time limit for this test, so I took a moment to close my eyes and tried to relax. In that moment of silence, it occurred to me that I had not prayed about the test. Although I still was not convinced that it would do any good, I could use all the help I could get. "I can't do this alone," I whispered. "I really need you, God." After several seconds had passed, I opened my eyes and read the first question.

Although the words that I read were familiar, the answer did not come to me. *Don't panic. Move on to the next question and relax.* Each time I read a new question, my mind was blank. All of this information had been taught to me during my training, yet it seemed to be locked away inside my brain, and I couldn't find the key.

I decided to move on to a different section of the test. Perhaps I would have better luck with a different topic. My reaction to these questions was the same. I was unable to remember any of the answers.

Overcome with anxiety, I wanted to quit. I was convinced that everything I had worked for was now lost. In my efforts to remember the answers, my heart beat faster with each moment that passed. The intense pounding within my chest became an audible thumping that echoed in my ears. The more I worried, the more distraught I became.

Resting my head in my hands, I took a deep breath and slowly let it out. A peacefulness, like a wave of tranquility, passed through my body. Gradually the tension began to diminish. A warm and relaxing sensation penetrated my shoulders, moved down my arms, and into my hands. Not wanting to disrupt this wonderful feeling, I didn't move for several minutes. *Where is this feeling coming from?*

Quietly, I sat in my chair, open and vulnerable to anything else that might occur. Still aware of the importance of passing this test, I focused on maintaining this tranquil state, and remembered a prayer I had learned as a child. The words had been written on a large, gold candle that my parents kept on an end table in their living room. Year after year, I read this prayer without giving much thought to its meaning. It was the Serenity Prayer.

God grant me the serenity to accept the things I cannot change,
courage to change the things I can,
and the wisdom to know the difference.

These words touched me as they never had before. It seemed that they were telling me that I could not change what had happened to me or erase the fears the rape had created within me. I would need to accept them as a part of who I am and move on from there. *Is the memory of this prayer God's way of telling me to let go of my fears and give them to Him?* At that moment my wounds from the rape were so raw that I wasn't capable of surrendering my fears to Him. I wanted to trust Him, but how could I depend on someone who watched me suffer and did nothing?

I had always thought surrendering was a sign of weakness. Since my intruder had robbed me of my independence and ability to take control over my own life, I was initially reluctant to give anyone, including God, power over me.

During the assault, and now in the testing room, came an intense peaceful presence that was undeniable. In my heart, I believed it was God, but it was too painful to think that He was with me but not helping me. It seemed as though He played the part of a spectator. *If this is really God, why doesn't He help?*

As I lifted my head, the calm presence lingered with me. Looking down at the test on the table, my eyes focused on the question at the top of the page. The soothing calm stayed with me. Slowly, I began reading the words. My eyes widened. I could clearly understand the meaning of the question! My thoughts returned to the training class. I picked up my pencil and wrote down the answer. My confidence soared! I was certain that I had answered the question correctly. Without hesitating, I continued reading. It was as if I had suddenly found the key that unlocked my memory and allowed me to retrieve the answers. Unsure of how long this period of clear thinking would last, I worked as fast as I could. Surprisingly, for many of the questions that followed, I was able to close my eyes and visualize the part of my notes where the correct answer was written. Although I still struggled through certain parts of the exam, I was overjoyed that I was able to write an answer for each question. It was almost four o'clock when I finally finished. Lisa was sitting at her desk as I approached.

"You were alone in that room a long time!" she exclaimed, as I handed her the completed test.

In my heart, I knew that she was wrong. I had not been alone.

"I'll try to correct it before we go home today. A manager will also need to take a look at it." I knew she was talking about our boss, Jeff.

"Thanks, Lisa," I said in appreciation.

As I walked back to the computer room, I realized that much of the tension I had carried with me throughout the week had disappeared. This amazing transformation allowed my thoughts to travel beyond my fears. The stress of preparing for the test was now behind me, and I was thinking more clearly. *God grant me the serenity to accept the things I cannot change . . .*

Not only had I been angry with my assailant, but I was also angry at myself for letting the fear and tension control me. Now, I would do my best to accept my feelings as a normal response to being raped. Maybe I could manage these feelings more effectively if I stopped fighting them. Perhaps my weaknesses were nothing to be ashamed of, and if I turned to God, he could help me turn them into strengths. I wondered if surrendering my problems to Him might even give me a sense of freedom. Although I still didn't know whether or not I had passed the test, my anxiety faded. Even if I were to lose my job, I felt strong enough to live with the consequences.

During the next half hour, I obsessively watched the clock. *Will Lisa finish checking my test before our shift ends at four thirty?* Waiting until Monday would be unbearable. I was just getting ready to walk over to her desk when the door to the computer room burst open. Lisa entered the room with a tremendous smile on her face. Seeing her expression, I felt my own excitement building. "You passed!" Lisa yelled, as she waved my test papers in the air. Seconds later she was hugging me with a strength I never knew she possessed. Unrestrained tears streamed freely down my cheeks. *I passed! How is it possible?* A tremendous burden had been lifted. *What is happening to me?* My experience during the test was the second time this peaceful, calming presence had enveloped me in the midst of despair. *Is this how God responds to us when we call? Is it our soul that hears Him first, then sending the message to our mind and body? Have I spent most of my life ignoring these messages? Why am I aware of them now? If it is through our souls that we experience His love and compassion, does God feel my emotions in the same way? Did He experience my anguish during the rape, and now my joy at having passed the test?* Although I had originally felt that God was a spectator during the rape, I now wondered. *Did He suffer as much as I did?* These questions flooded my thoughts on the way home from work that day. I realized it had been weeks since I had experienced a good night's sleep. I wanted nothing more than to go home and relax. When I pulled up to my house, there were no other cars in the driveway. My fears resurfaced, and I must have been an odd sight to my neighbors as I sat in my car, alone and paralyzed, waiting for Joanne to come home.

TWELVE

MY MISSION:
BECOME WHOLE AGAIN

As I sat waiting, I was aware of my extreme anger, mostly at the police department. Detective Shanahan had told me that the chances of the rapist returning were slim, but I was not reassured. The police hadn't shared with me the details of their investigation, and I erroneously believed they were doing nothing to find my assailant. I was angry at myself for my inability to recover from this trauma. I felt guilty for not having visible wounds resulting from the rape. *Is it possible that I didn't fight hard enough?* If the rapist had left more bruises, I'd have an excuse for my inability to cope. I reasoned that visual signs of the terror I had experienced might help others understand what I was going through. I was even angry with my parents for what I believed was their over-protectiveness, yet I continued to call them when Joanne was not around. My dependence on them was humiliating.

As if anger and guilt weren't enough, I was also experiencing intense loneliness, even when surrounded by friends, family, or coworkers. Good friends like Bernadette often called me to ask how I was doing, but it didn't take away the feelings of isolation that I continuously felt.

I thought of Gary. He had not called me since I told him what had happened. *Is the reason for this loneliness a result of his distance, both physically and emotionally? Or is it because no one seems to truly understand what I am feeling or know what they can do to help me?*

Never before had I considered counseling or other professional help for my problems. Sitting in the car, waiting, it became clear that I needed it now. The terrifying realization that my life could end at any time without a moment's notice was overwhelming and all-consuming. Yes, I was alive and breathing, but when the assailant left my house, part of my spirit went with him—the part that trusted my instincts and knew which feelings were rational and which ones were irrational. Although I did not consider suicide, I could understand why some choose that option when they can no longer experience happiness. If I had been killed, my anguish would have been over. The burden I was carrying would destroy me if I didn't get help. It was now my mission to become whole once again—to be able to experience joy in my daily life—to take back what had been stolen from me.

About fifteen minutes later, Joanne parked her car next to mine. Pretending as if I had just returned from work, I opened my door and stepped out.

In the house, I excitedly told Joanne about the results of my test and asked about her day. Then I went to my room and drifted off to sleep. It seemed like only a few minutes had gone by when Gary called. I was happy to hear from him, but somewhat apprehensive to talk to him.

Gary reminded me that he would be in Michigan the following weekend when we would be attending the wedding of a mutual friend. I felt hopeful that he would be more supportive when we saw each other. Then, when he told me that his visit to Michigan would only be twenty-four hours long, I felt betrayed. *Can't he find one extra day to spend with me?* He explained that he could not afford to take any time off work. It was becoming clear that he was not going to provide me with the emotional support that I needed, whether he stayed one day, a week, or an entire month! I suspected that my emotional instability made him uneasy, and that he thought that I had been "damaged."

On Saturday, I found myself alone in my house for the first time since the rape. Bravely, I had told Joanne and Sean that I was comfortable being by myself. With a smile on my face, I waved goodbye as they walked out the door. Two minutes later, fear overwhelmed me. With my back against the front door, I sat on the floor in the living room and waited anxiously for one of them to return. I realized that it was time to act on my earlier decision to get help. Moving away from the door just long enough to grab the telephone, I called the police department, and asked for the name of a support group that specialized in victims of rape. I was given the phone number to HAVEN (Help Against Violent Encounters Now), a local shelter for victims of domestic violence and sexual assault. Without putting down the receiver, I dialed the number and made an appointment to talk to a counselor.

THIRTEEN

An Angel to Watch Over Me

O n Sunday, I had dinner with my parents and we discussed ways to alleviate my anxiety. They suggested getting a dog. *Will I be home enough hours in the day to provide for a pet? Will Joanne's cat, Brandy, accept a new dog in the house?* After weighing all of the advantages and disadvantages of owning a pet, I decided that feeling safe was the top priority. Having a dog would be like having my own guardian angel to protect me.

Monday morning was the beginning of my second week back at work. The minute I saw Lisa, I told her about my thoughts of getting a dog. Lisa, not one to sit back and slowly mull things over, didn't surprise me by her response. "Great idea! We can look for one after work today." Searching through the phone book, we found a listing for an animal shelter located along the I-75 expressway. Lisa dialed the number, and after a brief conversation, hung up the phone and squealed with delight, "They're open till six o'clock!"

At four thirty sharp, Lisa and I headed toward the parking garage, not waiting for the rest of our coworkers who normally walked with us. Ten minutes later, we pulled into the parking lot of the animal shelter, where a pleasant woman named Carol led us into a large room with rows of dogs in cages, some barking excitedly. "I need to find a good watchdog," I told her. "I'd prefer a larger dog between one and three years old. It would be great if it is housebroken."

"The approximate age of each dog is listed on the pink index card hanging on each cage," Carol responded. "All that we know about each dog is also written there. Why don't you look around for a while and give me a shout if you have any questions."

During the next half hour, Lisa and I walked up and down the aisles of cages. Carrying a small notepad and pen, I scribbled information about each dog that I thought would make a good pet. Most of them looked at me with longing in their eyes. Each one wagged its tail as if to say, "Pick me!" When I finished, there were seven dogs on my list.

"How do I know which one would be the best watchdog?" I wondered out loud.

Lisa responded, "What would you like me to do, Julie? Walk up to each cage and growl? Maybe the one that growls back would be the best guard dog!"

"Go ahead!" I dared her.

One by one, my good friend walked up to the cage of each dog I had listed, put her face close to the metal bars, and growled. The first five dogs responded by backing up into their cage farther and lowering their ears. I was beginning to lose hope that I would find the right dog as we walked up to the sixth cage. The dog behind the bars was a large, chocolate Labrador mix. She had an adorable face and she sat quietly as we approached her. Lisa took a deep breath, looked directly into the dog's eyes, and growled loudly. Without hesitating, this beautiful Labrador charged the door of her cage and growled right back! "This is the one, Julie! She would never let anyone into your house. Take her home!"

Speechless, I took a closer look at the pink card hanging on the outside of her cage. It said, "Hello. My name is Angel."

Gingerly, I knelt down on the old tile floor in front of Angel's cage. A look of apprehension in her eyes, she had returned to her original position in the back of her cage. Her eyes shifted between Lisa's and mine, not knowing whether she could trust me. "Terrific! She'll probably never let me in your house now," said Lisa with a chuckle.

"Smart dog," I responded, unable to pass up an opportunity to tease Lisa.

We found Carol, who lifted the latch on the cage door and stood back to give me room to greet my new friend. Slowly, I extended my right hand toward Angel. Maybe I should have been leery about approaching this strange dog, yet I was not afraid. When she saw my hand reaching in her direction, her ears lowered and her tail began to nervously dust the floor behind her. Apparently, Angel was not yet willing to trust the friend of someone who had growled at her.

A full minute passed before this beautiful dog walked cautiously to me. Our eyes met and both of us, it seemed, forgot that Lisa and Carol were still in the room. We were drawn to each other, and before I even touched her, I sensed a bond between us.

"Angel," I sang out softly as she moved close enough to sniff my hand. Then she sat and allowed me to pet her. This brave but cautious dog seemed eager to go home with someone she could trust. Gently I stroked the top of her head and slid my hand down her long silky ears. Her tail began to move faster as she leaned her head into the hand that was petting her. It was at this moment that I had an extraordinary feeling that I had found the dog that I was supposed to find. *Is it just an amazing coincidence that her name is Angel?* An angel's purpose is to guard and enlighten. This dog, I believed, could offer me the protection and peace of mind that I so desperately needed. Eagerly, I turned and addressed Carol. "When can I take her home?"

"There is a short adoption process that needs to happen before we can let you take her." Carol held Angel's collar with her right hand and ushered her back through the open door of her cage. Reluctantly, Angel obeyed. With a troubled look in her eyes, she watched us walk away.

"Don't worry, Angel. I'll be back for you," I tried to reassure her.

At Carol's desk, she handed me a clipboard with a list of questions to answer. The shelter wanted to know the size of my house and yard, where my new pet would sleep, the hours I worked, and who else lived in the house. *What if they reject me because of the number of hours I work? Or the small size of my house and yard?*

When I handed the clipboard back to Carol, she told me that if my application to adopt Angel was approved, I could pick her up on the way home from work the next day. A feeling of excitement swept through me and the cloud of gloom that had been hovering over me lifted for a brief moment. As Lisa and I left the animal shelter, I felt grateful for Lisa's friendship. If it wasn't for her enthusiasm, I don't know if Angel and I would have found each other.

The next morning, Tuesday, I went to work with the anticipation of bringing home a second pair of eyes to stand on guard for me at night while I slept. The morning seemed to drag on forever, but in the afternoon I called the shelter. In the back of my mind, I was worried that they would reject me based on my busy lifestyle. At this point, it would have been a devastating blow. When I got Carol on the line, she said, "You can pick her up any time before six o'clock."

Overjoyed, I blurted out, "I'll be there before five o'clock. Thank you!" Hanging up the phone, I thought I might explode if I didn't find Lisa to tell her the good news. Rushing out of the computer room door, it didn't take long for me to find her in the office of the administrative assistant.

Excusing my interruption, I whispered in Lisa's ear, "They said that I can take Angel home today!"

"Great! Would you like some company when you pick her up?"

At four thirty Lisa and I were on our way to the shelter. Within ten minutes of arriving, I was holding a leash, and on the other end was my new found friend, Angel. Without any hesitation, she followed me, tail wagging, as if she had walked with me a thousand times. Lisa and I led her into the parking lot and directed her into the back seat of my car. As Lisa walked to her car, she said, "Good luck with Angel, Julie. I'll bet she's a terrific dog!"

"I never would have found her without you," I said with misty eyes.

"Yeah, I know!" Lisa said with a self-assured wink. "See you tomorrow!" She drove away.

In my car, I took a few moments to look behind me. Angel was lying peacefully on the blanket I had placed on the back seat. She lifted her head and looked at me as if to say, "I'm ready. Let's go home!"

Fastening my seat belt, I glanced over to the passenger seat, and the pink index card that had been hanging on Angel's cage caught my eye.

Carol must have handed it to me along with the rest of Angel's paper-work. Attached to the pink card was a white piece of paper that I hadn't noticed earlier. It said: "Angel is housebroken, good with kids, but not compatible with cats." *How in the world did I overlook this?* This could be a problem for Joanne's cat, Brandy! Not only was I bringing a strange dog into "her" house, but also one that didn't like cats! "Please behave your-self," I cautioned Angel as I began driving home. She looked at me as if she understood exactly what I meant.

At home, Joanne's car was in the driveway. Unable to avoid the meeting with Brandy any longer, I led Angel up the porch steps. Taking a deep breath, I opened the door and let Angel in. Excitedly, she pranced from room to room, making new discoveries with every step. So I wouldn't startle Joanne I called out to her from the living room, "I'm home . . . and I'm not alone!"

"I'll be right out," Joanne shouted. Seconds later, she emerged from her bedroom with Brandy at her heels. Instantly, Brandy noticed the large, strange animal at the end of the leash I was holding. Her eyes widened. Angel noticed Brandy, too. They were careful not to make any sudden moves toward each other.

"Well, hello there!" Joanne exclaimed as she walked farther into the living room. "You must be Angel." Angel's tail wagged furiously when she heard her name, and Joanne reached over to pat her head.

"I just love her, Joanne. Thanks for agreeing to another pet. It's great to know that I will never have to walk into an empty house."

"No problem, Julie. She'll help me feel more comfortable, too."

Although Brandy spent most of her time hiding from Angel during the next few days, she gradually became used to having a dog around the house. I never did figure out why Angel's paperwork claimed that she didn't like cats. When Joanne and I were around, Brandy would act like Angel was a nuisance. Yet, we would often catch a glimpse of them hanging out together as we peered through the front window before entering our house. Their antics would be the source of many humorous stories during their years with us.

Joanne was in a hurry to leave for her part-time job at a local bowling alley. Sean was still staying with us, although he wasn't home yet. It was a warm, fall evening, perfect for taking a stroll through the neighborhood. Lately, I had been afraid to walk by myself, but having Angel with me gave me renewed courage.

I put Angel on the collar and leash I had purchased the previous evening. We left the house with no specific route in mind. We were about a half mile from home when I noticed someone approaching me from the other direction. I began to panic. This was clearly a *man,* and suddenly I was afraid of him. He was walking a dog that was slightly larger than Angel. Hastily, I decided it would be a good idea to cross the street in order to avoid him. As I waited for traffic to clear, I saw that the man was walking with a white cane. *Is this man blind?*

When he was about fifteen feet away, he suddenly began talking to me. "Excuse me. Can you tell me where I am?"

How does this man know that I'm here if he can't see? Is he really blind? "Pardon me?" was all I could think of to say. Angel was pulling me towards him, determined to get closer to the stranger's dog.

"I need to get to Nine Mile and Woodward Avenue. Can you tell me how far away that is?"

This man was more that two miles from where he wanted to be. Still keeping a safe distance from him, I nervously gave him directions. "You are walking in the wrong direction, sir. To get to Nine Mile and Woodward, you need to travel about one mile south and one and a half miles west."

A look of sheer frustration appeared on his face and I heard him curse his dog under his breath. My first instinct was to say, "Don't worry, stay right here and I'll get my car so I can drive you." Yet these words would not leave my mouth. Afraid to trust this blind man, I watched him as he turned around slowly and began his long walk along the busy road.

I darted home, crying uncontrollably. Without hesitation, Angel loped beside me. Before the rape I never would have ignored the plight of this man. I was angry with myself and the rapist. *How can I stand back and watch a blind man try and find his way?* It had been my hope that bringing Angel into my house would magically erase all of my worries and fears. The depth of my trauma was becoming even more apparent.

To my relief, I saw my dad's car parked on the side of my house. Bursting through the front door, I struggled through my tears to explain what had just happened. My father's gentle nature soothed me in this moment as it had throughout my entire life. He calmly asked me, "Would you like to go with me in my car and see if we can find him?"

We spent the next hour driving up and down every road in the area looking for the blind man. We never did find him. *Was I too paranoid, or did I make a sensible decision based on my intuition?* I couldn't tell. *What if he accidentally took another wrong turn, or worse yet, was hit by a car?* Here I was, making so many demands on the people in my life, yet I was incapable of helping someone else in need! *Perhaps it's a good thing to be leery of strangers. But if that is true, why do I feel as though I have lost something incredibly precious? Will I spend the rest of my life closing my eyes to the needs of strangers out of fear?*

Joanne arrived home from her job at the bowling alley shortly after eleven p.m. Sean was with her. Exhausted after a long day, she went directly into the bathroom to get ready for bed. In an attempt to put Angel at ease, I sat down on my own bed and called her over to the soft blanket I had placed on the floor next to the bed.

"Lie down, girl," I pleaded softly. Without hesitating, Angel walked over to the blanket, turned around in one complete circle, and let out a tired groan as she lay down next to my bed. Putting my head on the pillow, I dangled my arm over the edge of my mattress and stroked the short, silky fur on Angel's head. I looked forward to sleeping peacefully for a change, and I hoped that Angel would instinctively bark if she heard any unusual noise.

Exhausted, I began drifting off to sleep within minutes. Apparently, Angel enjoyed the attention, because when I stopped petting her, she began to whine. "Oh great! What do I do now?" I grumbled, hoping she didn't expect me to stay up all night with her. Gently, I began stroking her fur again. Her whining stopped. Once again, sleep overtook me, and Angel protested with her cries. Each time I would fall asleep, Angel would whine. I became worried that we were keeping Joanne and Sean awake. In desperation, I picked up Angel's blanket from the floor and put it up on the bed near my feet. "Come on up, Angel," I sighed wearily. She jumped onto the blanket. For the rest of that night, and every night for the rest of her life, she slept peacefully on the foot of my bed.

Although Angel's presence provided me with protection and comfort in the aftermath of the rape, her presence did not alleviate my constant worry that something dreadful was about to happen.

FOURTEEN

More Losses

Saturday afternoon, Gary arrived at my home in a black Lincoln Town Car that he had rented. Nervously, I studied his tall, slender physique as he strode up the sidewalk to my house. The Florida sun had darkened his skin and turned his hair several shades lighter—almost blond. He looked especially handsome in his dark suit and tie. Before he could reach my front porch, I stepped out to greet him. When our eyes met, he seemed to quicken his pace and reached me in a matter of seconds. Wrapping his arms around me, he embraced me with all the warmth that I remembered from the past. Just for the moment, it felt like he had never moved to Florida, and that nothing had changed. Yet, as he released his hug, the reality of our situation came flooding back, and I suddenly did not trust that the affection he was showing me was authentic. His eyes appeared to be looking past me, possibly avoiding the hurt in my eyes. "How are you, sweet stuff?" he greeted me in his usual, cheerful manner.

"Good, Gary. How 'bout yourself?"

"All right, I guess." It appeared that neither Gary nor I were comfortable talking about anything other than superficial pleasantries at the moment. I invited him in to talk to Joanne while I grabbed my purse and sweater.

Before we left, Joanne asked if she could take a picture of us. We stood next to the grandfather clock, and Gary put his arm loosely around my waist. Many years later, when looking at that picture, I noticed that we had positioned ourselves in the exact spot where the rape took place. *What a strange coincidence. Was it an accident that we chose that specific location to pose for the picture? Did I associate the feeling of being betrayed by Gary with the tragedy that had happened in that spot a few weeks earlier?* It is still uncomfortable for me to look at that photograph.

Joanne took another picture of us outside, standing by the rental car. After opening the passenger door for me, Gary walked around to the driver's side and sat beside me in the front seat. It was just the two of us now, and it was a forty-five-minute drive to the wedding reception. It was our first opportunity to talk to each other face to face about our relationship and what we were feeling. Neither of us seemed to know what to say. Gary was normally candid and straightforward when talking about his feelings, yet now he kept them to himself. Gary never did share with me why he had become so distant.

During the wedding, Gary spent most of the time with other guests, and I struggled to talk to the people that I knew. *Is his behavior a coincidence, or is it intentional?* Although I had been looking forward to this wedding, I was now anxious to get home. Before the rape, I had been unaware of any changes in his feelings towards me. Now he was treating me like an acquaintance. *What is the real reason Gary is choosing this specific time to end our relationship?* I suspected that my friend, Nancy, was also avoiding me. Before the rape, she had been someone that I would see most weekends, meeting for dinner or bowling together on a league. The day of the rape, she had been put in the uncomfortable position of telling my father about my assault. Since then, I had only talked to her a couple of times. *Does what happened to me bother Gary and Nancy so deeply that they would rather avoid me than face me?*

My memory of the car ride home with Gary is filled with sadness. It was clear to me that he was a part of my past and wouldn't likely be a significant presence in my future. The loneliness that I experienced was overwhelming.

When we arrived at my house that night, Gary and I slowly walked up the narrow walkway to the front door. Standing on my porch, with the moon looking over our shoulders, Gary put his arms around me and kissed me goodnight. It could have been the stiffness in his hug, or possibly the expression on his face, but the message he was sending me was clear. The passion that had once existed in our relationship had vanished. The last thing I remember is watching him disappear into the black Lincoln he had left idling in the street. There was no doubt in my mind that this was the last time I would ever feel Gary's embrace.

FIFTEEN

A Safe HAVEN

On Tuesday evening, September 16, I had my first appointment at HAVEN. The half-hour trip to Pontiac passed quickly, and I soon found myself in front of a building with an address matching the one I had written down. I was confused when I did not see a HAVEN sign on the front of the red brick building, so I double-checked the address before pulling into the parking lot. I noticed a small, fenced playground adjacent to the building. Sadness came over me as I realized that the children who played here had probably fled homes struck by violence.

Standing in the parking lot, I scanned the building for the entry door, but I saw only windows. As I walked around the property, I noticed a large metal door on the side of the old building. Oddly, the door was missing a doorknob, or any kind of outside handle. I finally noticed a doorbell located to the right of the door, and pressed the button. Within seconds, a short-haired woman with glasses peered through a small rectangular window in the door. "Can I help you?" she asked politely, opening the door just enough for me to see her face.

"Yes, I have an appointment with Jackie. Do I have the right place?" I asked with uneasiness.

"Yes you do. Please come in, and I'll let her know you're here."

Jackie was an attractive young woman who appeared to be in her mid-thirties. She invited me to share why I had come to HAVEN. For the remainder of our session, she seldom talked, but appeared to be listening closely to my words. It felt good to talk about the rape without being afraid of disturbing or hurting someone I loved, yet something didn't feel right. Jackie seemed to be an understanding woman, but I felt a tremendous need to speak with someone who had lived through the same trauma that I had. I expressed this to Jackie. Her facial expression suggested that I had hurt her feelings, but she nodded and told me about a support group of women who were victims of rape. They met every Thursday at HAVEN to share their stories, fears, sorrows, frustrations, and healing. This was my first and last meeting with Jackie.

For the next six months, I faithfully made the thirty-minute trip to HAVEN each Thursday evening after work. Although the first meeting was a bit tense, I knew immediately that I was in the right place. There were six other women present, sitting on chairs and an old, worn-out couch. The women appeared to range in age from their early twenties to their mid-fifties. I learned that some of them had been coming to this support group for several months, others only a few weeks. A few of them came to the meetings regularly, some attended only once. Each person's experience was different, thus their needs varied.

The facilitator identified herself as Marie and invited me to introduce myself. That first night, I didn't volunteer any additional information, and no one seemed to expect any from me. I listened to the frightening and tragic stories of the other women. One said that her rape had occurred twenty years ago, but she still felt the need to talk about it. *Is it possible that the effects of my rape may linger on for twenty years or more?* It was my hope that a year after my assault, my fears would be nothing but a distant memory.

Others told stories of violent sexual assaults where they were beaten until their faces were unrecognizable, and I felt blessed. Some told stories of being raped by family members, and I felt grateful that my attacker was a stranger. Women who knew their attacker were often blamed for what had happened to them. Although people in my life had accused me of being careless, they never suggested that it was my fault that I was raped. Society, I believe, has a tendency to want to blame the victims of rapists for what has happened to them. If women believe that victims of sexual assault acted a certain way or dressed provocatively and it caused them to be raped, they could convince themselves that something like that could never happen to them.

During that first meeting and the ones that followed, I continued to learn more about the crime of rape. From my own experience, I already suspected that men who rape aren't motivated by sexual pleasure. The facilitator verified this presumption. The purpose of the attack is to control their victims. They choose women they perceive as being vulnerable and easy prey. It doesn't matter whether they are attractive or not, heavy or thin, old or young. In the process of dominating and hurting their victims, they gain a sense of power and control that they are unable to obtain elsewhere.

There were many common threads among the members of the group. The loss of control that was felt at the time of the assault seemed to linger. Following an attack, each day was a challenge to regain control over their emotions and fears. Another common thread was depression. Some women described the days and weeks following the rape as being an emotional roller coaster, never knowing what might trigger an episode of uncontrollable weeping or bouts of anxiety. Others were unable to concentrate while at work; some lost their jobs and faced financial hardship. Several talked about their inability to return to work on a regular basis. They began calling in sick and were unable to tell their employers the real reason for their sudden change in behavior.

Some women felt that they could no longer trust men, especially the ones that physically resembled their attackers. Several married women expressed their inability to enjoy sexual relations after they had been raped. Since I believed that rape was not a sexual act, I hoped it would not affect my attitude toward sex. Yet I was unsure if memories of the rapist's actions would come flooding back to me during a future intimate relationship.

Soon, I realized that the women in this particular support group could be divided into two categories: those that wanted to forget about the rape and not talk about it, and those, like myself, who needed to talk about it in order to lessen the pain. The women in both categories were angry at their rapists. They expressed their anger in varying degrees, many of them projecting it onto other people in their lives. Some were upset at family members and friends who did not understand what they were going through or blamed them for being raped.

Others, like me, were angry because they felt the authorities were not trying hard enough to catch the perpetrator. Each week I would call Detective Shanahan in an attempt to find out whether she was making any progress with my case. I believed that if I didn't call occasionally, I might never hear from her again. Often, Detective Shanahan did not return my calls. During one of our phone conversations, I remember telling her, "I just need reassurance that the police department hasn't forgotten about me and given up looking for him."

For a moment there was silence on her end of the line. Then, in a voice without expression, she said, "We'll let you know if there is any news." I interpreted this to mean they were doing nothing. *This criminal is going to remain free to rape other women.*

Detective Shanahan's apparent lack of compassion made it difficult for me to trust her, but it was not her fault that I was raped. Apparently, it was her way of dealing with the disturbing cases she worked on. If she focused on the emotion, she might be swept away by the same feelings as the victim. Erroneously, I believed that if people couldn't feel my pain, they wouldn't be effective in helping me.

Little was said about anger towards God in the support group, although it was on my mind quite often. I was mad at God for doing nothing to stop the assault, yet I was ashamed to admit it. Unable to face this guilt, I avoided going to church most Sundays. It seemed like I had enough to worry about and didn't want to dwell on these thoughts.

Up until this time, I had spoken little about my anger toward the man that had attacked me. Fear of him seemed to weave its way into every moment of the day, most of the time refusing to step aside and make room for anger or any other emotion. The face of the rapist, distorted by the stocking over his head, looked more like a monster to me than a man. When we think of demons, we feel fright and horror, not anger.

While attending HAVEN's support group, I felt safe, and I was able to see beyond these feelings of terror. It became possible to feel anger toward my assailant, thus relieving the animosity I felt toward people that didn't deserve it. My attacker was a human being that made the conscious decision to break into my house and wait quietly in Joanne's closet until I woke. Not only did I want him caught—I wanted him dead!

At each meeting I attended, a sense of loss seemed to permeate the members' feelings. The sadness from these losses was etched on each of our faces. Part of the sorrow came from the dependence on friends and family to provide a feeling of safety or to provide financial help. This inability to bounce back and regain our independence was depressing.

Those who were attacked by strangers had feared, as I did, that they would be murdered when the rapist was finished with his torment. I was surprised to learn that many women who had faced death during their rapes were no longer afraid to die. *Did their thoughts turn to family and God as a means of escaping the horror of the moment?* I never asked.

Gradually, HAVEN's support group helped me see beyond my fears, and allowed me to understand all of the mixed emotions that I was feeling. Talking to others with similar experiences helped lessen the feeling of isolation, and I learned that my thoughts and fears were completely normal for someone who had lived through the trauma of rape. Most women that had experienced a vicious attack or home intrusion were afraid to be alone in their houses. Many of them feared that their attackers would return. My sense of security had been stolen from me, and the support group helped me to realize that it was going to take time to gain it back.

At HAVEN, I never worried that I was bothering anyone when I vented my concerns. Each week, these women encouraged me to take control over my life and to voice my concerns to the detective responsible for my case. It was at their suggestion that I eventually wrote a letter to the Royal Oak police chief describing how I felt. The process of writing the letter was an opportunity to let the police department know that I was a real person, not just a case number to be put away on a shelf.

With my family and friends, I avoided the subject of rape most of the time. Believing that the people who were close to me were tired of hearing about it, I kept my feelings to myself after the first couple of months that followed the assault. My friends rarely brought up the subject.

This experience taught me a valuable lesson. When we suffer a loss or experience a tragedy, memories of our experience may dominate our thoughts for a long time. Often, loved ones think that if they don't bring up the subject or ask about our misfortune, we won't be reminded of it. They would be surprised to learn that those of us who have been wounded are constantly thinking about our loss. The people who invite us to share our concerns often give us great comfort. When someone I know is in pain, I always try to remember this truth.

The counselors at HAVEN were the first to introduce me to the concept of becoming empowered. It is the recognition that within each of us lies the power to overcome adversity. Empowerment, to me, is the discovery that God is within me, giving me the strength I need to cope with all hardships that occur in my life. I learned that my interaction with other individuals helped to unlock that power inside of me. The personal stories of courage and perseverance that I heard from the women at HAVEN inspired me and taught me about the indestructible power of the human spirit.

HAVEN stressed the importance of defining ourselves as *survivors* instead of *victims*. It would be a while before I would feel like a survivor, but at least I was pointed in the right direction.

Several months into our sessions, I noticed a new confidence developing within me that I had not possessed before the rape. Most of my life I had been somewhat shy and remained quiet during conversations among groups of people. Sharing my story was something I now found easier to do. I did not realize that the confidence I gained at HAVEN would soon be needed.

SIXTEEN

AN UNEXPECTED MISSION

During October 1986, my mother was enrolled in a criminal justice class at the University of Detroit. Her professor, Dr. Isaiah "Ike" McKinnon, asked his students if they knew of a friend or family member who had been victimized. He was interested in having someone speak to the class about their experience. Although she thought about mentioning the rape, my mom felt uneasy about volunteering me for something I might not be ready to do. She said nothing to her class, but the following evening, she called me at home to tell me about her professor's request. Although the thought of speaking publicly had never crossed my mind, surprisingly I thought it was something I would like to do. This would be a huge challenge for me, yet I saw it as an opportunity to have something positive come from my tragic situation.

A week later, I received a phone call from Ike McKinnon. He asked if we could meet ahead of time to discuss my presentation to his class. Since it had only been eight weeks since my rape, he wanted to make sure that both he and I were comfortable with what he was asking me to do. He suggested that we have lunch later that week at one of the restaurants in the Renaissance Center where I worked.

As I approached the restaurant, I recognized Dr. McKinnon almost immediately from the description he had given me earlier, that included his dark-blue sport coat. He had a commanding presence, broad shoulders, and was leaning back in his chair, his long legs extended into the aisle between the tables. He looked up as I approached, then stood up and extended his hand. "You must be Julie," he said, smiling warmly. As I looked up into the soft eyes of this handsome black man, my nervousness faded.

"Yes I am," I responded, reaching to shake his hand. He was much taller than I had expected. "It's a pleasure to meet you, Dr. McKinnon."

"We spent the next few minutes getting acquainted and ordering lunch before discussing the presentation for his class. His calm and gentle nature put me at ease as we talked about each of our backgrounds. Ike McKinnon was director of public safety and adjunct professor of criminal justice at the University of Detroit. He had worked for many years at various jobs in the Detroit Police Department, including an assignment as lieutenant in charge of the sex crimes unit.

Several people in the restaurant recognized him, and stopped to say hello. He responded to them politely, yet continued to listen to me without being distracted. When our lunch arrived, we continued talking. Our conversation was lighthearted and comfortable up to this point, so I was surprised when he suddenly looked up and said, "Tell me what happened."

His question caught me off guard, and it felt as though I had been kicked in the stomach. "Are you asking me to tell you about the rape?" My voice trembled. No one had asked me that question since the morning the police officers and detectives had talked to me. Once again, it was a law officer who talked easily and openly about sexual assault and invited me to do the same.

Although I started out a bit shaky, I was able to calmly tell him about that horrific morning that my house was broken into. As he had done earlier, Dr. McKinnon listened carefully to every word that I said. His deep interest in my experience made me believe that I had an important message to communicate. *Is it possible that others might benefit by listening to my story?*

Ike McKinnon believed that his class would benefit. He wanted to put an actual face on the victims of violent crimes. In that way, his students would understand that victims are real people—not just stories in newspapers or on television. One of the most memorable things that he shared with me was, "Whenever the victim's actions or courageous response to a crime receives more attention than the criminal himself, it is an inspiration to all of us." By the time we had finished lunch, we were both comfortable with the idea of me talking to his class.

My stomach was in knots, my heart was pounding, and my hands were trembling as I stood in front of Professor McKinnon's University of Detroit classroom and surveyed the group of about twenty criminal justice students waiting for me to speak. Several of the students were police officers who had contact with victims of violent crimes on a regular basis.

Seconds earlier, Professor McKinnon had introduced me to his class as a survivor of a sexual assault. Looking for guidance, I prayed quietly, then began to speak. Soon, I realized that only a couple of students were looking at me, and one of them was my mother! *Are they even listening to me? Or do they find it difficult to look directly into the eyes of a sexual assault victim?* In an attempt to get their attention, I spoke louder, yet most of the class was still looking at the floor or out of the window.

Discouraged, but not willing to give up, I was determined to help my audience understand this crime by describing the thoughts and emotions that I experienced during the attack. I shared with them that the actions that I was subjected to were done angrily, violently, and against my will. It was intolerable torture, and there was nothing I could do to stop my assailant. Yet, the most painful part of the experience was believing that he would kill me. It was unbearable to think about the impact it would have on my loved ones, finding my nude body spread on the floor with my hands tied behind my back.

My next comments were directed at the police officers that I knew were in the audience. It was important that they know that the first person that a victim comes into contact with after an assault has a significant influence on how the victim will view herself and her recovery. If treated with compassion and understanding, she will be less likely to blame herself or feel that she has done anything wrong. Police officers who are patient and treat emotionally distraught victims with empathy will have more cooperative witnesses.

At the end of my talk, I breathed a sigh of relief. *Did they listen to me? Do they understand my message? Did I change their attitude about rape and its victims?* As I surveyed the room, I was aware that each of the students was looking directly at me. I had my answers. My mission had begun.

From one side of the room, I noticed a student push herself away from her desk and slowly stand. It was my mother. "The speaker is my daughter," she said proudly, her eyes welling up with tears.

Ike McKinnon asked me to speak several more times to his classes. With each opportunity, I felt more confidence in my ability to change attitudes, raise public awareness, and to somehow make it easier for other rape victims to speak openly about the violent crimes that were committed against them.

I drew strength from my speaking engagements. And I drew strength from Ike McKinnon. He had experienced more violence and witnessed more crimes than anyone I had ever met, yet he was living his life without anger or resentment. As a teenager growing up in Detroit, he was beaten by a white police officer. As a young man, he spent time in Vietnam during the 1960s. Then he was a rookie police officer during the 1967 Detroit riots and experienced a great deal of racism. He survived stabbings and being shot at, yet he kept a positive attitude, thankful for the negative experiences in his life.

After his beating by the white police officer, he vowed that he would make his career in law enforcement and try to eliminate the brutality that he had experienced. Years later, as a patrol officer, he saw the officer who had beaten him sitting in a restaurant. At first he stormed toward him, "ready to avenge the hurt, the pain, and the tears he had kept bottled up inside." The older man was unaware that this was the young boy he had once overpowered. When he saw Ike McKinnon standing at his table, he looked up and respectfully addressed him as "Officer." Ike suddenly felt all of his rage disappear. Instead of confronting him with anger, he just looked at the man's old, weather-beaten face and said, "A number of years ago you did something to me that changed my life."

The man was trembling now, looked back at Ike McKinnon and asked, "Tell me. What did I do?"

Calmly, Ike responded, "You won't remember what you did. You won't remember it at all. But you know something? I want to thank you for it." He then walked away, smiling. If he had never been beaten by the white police officer, he might never have become a police officer himself, devoting his life to protecting the Detroit community and inspiring others to do the same.

Dr. McKinnon gave me the opportunity to pursue my new mission. Soon, another caring man would hand me the knowledge that I could, once again, live free.

SEVENTEEN

A TASTE OF FREEDOM

At work, ever since the rape, Richard always asked how I was doing, and I felt safe confiding in him. Week after week he listened patiently while I lamented the loss of my independence and the all-consuming anxiety that my attacker could be stalking me. Richard believed that some of my stress would be alleviated if I spent time away from the place where the rape occurred. He repeatedly urged me to get away, suggesting places far from home.

Each time we talked, I found an excuse for not traveling. Usually, I mumbled something about vacations being too costly or how it would be difficult to leave Angel. The truth was that my fear of being alone kept me from leaving.

Richard refused to give up. He told me about his sister, Joyce, and her husband, who lived in a beautiful affluent neighborhood in Malibu, California, within walking distance of the Pacific Ocean. He suggested that I fly out to Southern California alone, rent a car, and stay at his sister's house for a week!

The idea of staying in the house of someone I had never met seemed ludicrous. *Why would his sister allow a total stranger to move in with her family for even a few days?* Relentless in his efforts to talk me into traveling, he told me more about Joyce's home each time he had the chance. Finally, out of sheer frustration, I told him to call her and ask if I would be welcome. Expecting her to say no, I was hoping this might alleviate the pressure that Richard was putting on me to travel.

Joyce said "Yes!" The kindness and generosity of Richard and his sister was astonishing. Once again, people I barely knew were willing to go out of their way to help me.

Less than a month later, in November, I was on a plane bound for Los Angeles. On my arrival, I rented a car and headed north to Malibu Beach to find the home of Richard's sister. I had never been to Southern California. I was more excited than nervous about this new adventure. The independence and freedom that I felt as I drove north was a tremendous relief from the suffocating fear, dependence, and anger that I had been living with since August. Suddenly, I was grateful for Richard's persistence in convincing me to travel. Now more than ever I was aware that bad things can happen to you any time and anywhere, but somehow I felt safer three thousand miles away from my own home. At least I knew that my attacker was not near me or watching me.

Before leaving Michigan, I had spoken to Richard's sister, Joyce, only once. She seemed warm and friendly on the phone as she explained that her daughter, Stacy, had agreed to let me stay in her room while she was away at school. She said that her husband, Earl, was also in agreement with her decision to let me stay. Our conversation was brief. She asked very few questions, and I was amazed at her trusting nature. We had never met, yet she was giving me a sanctuary to help me find the peace of mind that would allow me to feel *normal* again, if only for a few days.

As I neared Joyce and Earl's home that glorious day in mid-November, I looked out over the ocean from the Pacific Coast Highway. The magnificent, vast, blue water glistened under the brilliant rays of the afternoon sun, and it seemed strange to feel its warmth that late in the fall. I saw the name of Joyce's street and turned into the neighborhood. The homes that lined this street were large, sprawling ranches. They were beautifully landscaped, and it lifted my spirits to see all of the rich, green foliage. This shrubbery was in direct contrast to the barren branches that were evident in Michigan during November.

I pulled my rental car slowly into Joyce's driveway. Sitting in front of her home, I was suddenly overwhelmed with uncertainty. I knew almost nothing about this family whose house I was preparing to sleep in for the next five days. *What will I talk to her about?*

As it turned out, I had nothing to worry about. Joyce welcomed me into her home warmly and without reservation. She offered me a cup of tea, and we sat at her kitchen table and talked freely for over an hour.

Although I had expected her to look like her brother Richard, her light-brown hair with red highlights and smaller frame were in contrast to her brother's dark hair and stockier appearance. Yet the compassion that each of them exhibited toward me was the same. Once again, I was reminded of the many ways God intervenes in our lives.

During my stay in Southern California, I spent only brief periods of time within the confines of Joyce's house. Not wanting to be a burden to her family, I kept myself busy sightseeing and eating out.

Malibu became a relaxing retreat for me, a way of finding time alone and cherishing my freedom. Here I felt safe in public places, enjoying my independence without the worry that someone might attack me. My ability to successfully navigate the California expressways by myself and to locate the different attractions filled me with a self-confidence that I had never before experienced. It was the first time in my life that I felt comfortable eating alone in a restaurant. The trip taught me that I could enjoy my own company!

The excitement of the tourists that surrounded me was contagious, and I enjoyed myself immensely, alone and among strangers. During walks along the beach near Joyce's home, I remained aware of my surroundings—my shoulders would become tense if an unfamiliar man happened to walk by. Still, the rays of the magnificent California sun warmed my heart and quieted my fears. The feel of the smooth, white sand between my toes and the ocean's waves splashing against my feet helped me to remember that life still held many pleasures. As I listened to the lazy call of the seagulls, my thoughts became uncluttered and my fears more distant. Richard had been right. Getting away from my house and experiencing a feeling of independence was giving me hope. Finding peace and contentment again would be difficult, but not impossible.

One of my most pleasant memories of my visit to Malibu was lying in bed late at night and enjoying the moonlight filtering in through the wood shutters that covered the windows of Stacy's room. For the first time since the end of August, I was at peace, and free from fear that the rapist was parked in the street, watching my house. It was a wonderful feeling, and I took advantage of the situation by sleeping late each morning.

After I got back home to Michigan, I found myself craving those peaceful moments spent alone on that vacation, and I used their soothing memories to comfort me during stressful times. I continued to call Detective Shanahan to ask about progress on my case. Her cool demeanor became even more unpleasant during our phone conversations. Frustrated by the inability of the police department to find the perpetrator, I annoyed her with my frequent phone calls. Detective Shanahan kept me in the dark about any progress they were making, and I interpreted this to mean that they were doing nothing. My belief that there would be more victims continued to plague me and fuel my anger.

Apparently, God thought I needed a little more time away from my home, because three months later I was given another opportunity to travel, only this time it was work related. My manager called me into his office one day in early March. Our company was working with a major airline in Minneapolis, Minnesota to update one of their computer systems. Since I had operated the same type of equipment that the airline used in my work at the Renaissance Center, I was asked to work on this account in Minneapolis for six to eight weeks.

My first instinct was once again to say no, worried mostly about my dog, Angel, and the upkeep of my house. Since my manager had given me a couple of days to ponder this decision, I decided to talk with Joanne before making up my mind. She would have the responsibility of taking care of Angel each day and the maintenance of our home. It didn't seem fair to burden her with these responsibilities. To my surprise, Joanne didn't seem to mind. She volunteered Sean for the outdoor upkeep, and if there was a time that she would be gone for an extended period, she would ask for my parents' help with Angel.

My excuses melted away, and less than a week later, I found myself on an airplane headed for Minneapolis. Although I was apprehensive about working in an unfamiliar city with a group of people I didn't know, I was getting better at trusting that this was what God wanted me to do. In California, I had enjoyed the time that I had spent alone. Maybe my trip to Minnesota would also help me in my journey to regain my independence.

Initially, it appeared as though I misinterpreted God's plan for me. Maybe I was supposed to say no to this trip. The first two weeks of my assignment did not go as smoothly as I had hoped. Although the company provided me with a beautifully furnished apartment, staying completely alone at night turned out to be extremely nerve-wracking. In California, Richard's sister and her family were in the next room each night while I slept. In Minnesota, there was no one else. Most nights I fell asleep, exhausted, on the couch in front of the television. Although there was a bedroom with a comfortable bed in the rear of the apartment, I was afraid to sleep in it. It was my belief that I could be trapped in a back bedroom if anyone were to break in.

Within a week, it became clear that I did not have the experience that the manager of this account had hoped for. Therefore, I was not qualified to do the job I had been sent to do. My self-confidence plummeted, and my loneliness deepened. Frustrated, I believed I would be sent home early. Deep down, I hoped that would happen. Although my sense of security in my house had been tarnished, I still loved my home and wanted to be there. And regardless of whether I stayed in Minnesota or went home to Michigan, the independence and freedom that I had felt while in California seemed unattainable. Although it was difficult for me to let go of my worry, I had learned that praying about it would help.

After a couple of days of uncertainty, I was offered a different job on the same airline account. Apparently, Minnesota was where I belonged. The manager liked my ambition, and said that I maintained a positive attitude throughout my short stay. They needed someone to help track and record the percentage of airplane flights that were on time or delayed each week. With this information, my employer could better serve the client's needs and create the best automated system to track their flights. I would be working directly with the client's employees each morning beginning at six a.m. Even though I dreaded the early starting time, this job would keep me so busy that I wouldn't have time to dwell on my problems. I accepted the position.

Ellen, a woman from the Detroit area, would be my supervisor during the remainder of the time I worked on this account. My first impression was that she had an incredibly serious nature, and I was intimidated by her professionalism. However, it didn't take long for me to realize that she was easygoing with a great sense of humor. A friendship quickly developed between us, and suddenly I didn't feel as lonely. We often ate dinner together after a long day. When time permitted, we went shopping or sightseeing together. Without her friendship, the loneliness that usually results from working far from home would have been unbearable.

There was, however, one conversation between us that left me feeling uncomfortable and confused. Near the end of our stay, I confided in Ellen and told her about the sexual assault. During our conversation, I spoke about my anger and frustration due to the inability of the police department to find the man who had attacked me. I mentioned that if he was ever caught, I thought that he should spend the rest of his life in prison so he couldn't hurt anyone else. Then I asked her what she thought.

"A life sentence would be too long," was her response.

Surprised with her comment, I asked her what she meant. Ellen thought for a moment, and then responded, "Well . . . at least he didn't hurt you."

My eyes widened! I was stunned by her comment. If he didn't hurt me, why was I unable to cope with normal daily life? *Is this how the rest of society feels?*

Ellen's attitude was representative of legions of others. Although there were no physical scars, my soul continued to feel the agonizing pain of the violation. I would forever mourn the loss of the tranquility I once knew.

At the time of our conversation, I remember being upset with Ellen. However, her words turned out to be a blessing to me, inspiring me to continue my mission of speaking openly about the rape and educating others. My anger wasn't directed toward her as much it was toward a society that did not view rape as a serious crime.

The time that I spent on this temporary assignment had been extended from six weeks to almost four months. It wasn't until the first week in July that I was finally able to return to Michigan. The anticipation of sleeping in my own bed and being reunited with my dog, Angel, almost made me forget about the fear I associated with my Royal Oak house.

Staring out the window of the airplane, I was deep in thought during my entire flight home. *Do I feel any better now than I did four months ago? Am I truly more independent?* From one day to the next, or even from one week to the next, I would feel little improvement in my level of comfort. Looking back, there was no doubt that I had made progress in my recovery and in rediscovering my faith. However, on my return home, I didn't recognize it. It seemed as though there was no end in sight to my lingering fears. More help was on the way. This time, it would come by way of the Royal Oak Police Department. What was to happen next in my life was to be a shocking surprise.

EIGHTEEN

PRAYERS ANSWERED

I was driving home from work on a Thursday in mid-July. As I approached my home, I noticed my mom's car parked in the street and saw her sitting in the driver's seat. *That's strange. She usually calls before coming over.* When I pulled into the driveway, she stepped out of her car and hurried in my direction. She was holding a newspaper. "Hey, Mom. Is something wrong?" I called out as I got out of the car.

Coming closer, she held up the newspaper so I could see the front page. It was a copy of the *Royal Oak Daily Tribune.* The headline read, "Ann Arbor Suspect Linked to Area Rapes."

My adrenalin was pumping. *Does "area rapes" refer to rapes that happened in Royal Oak?* Ann Arbor is a city located about an hour west of Royal Oak. I scrutinized my mother's expression. "Are you thinking it's the same guy that broke into my house?"

"Read the article," Mom responded. Still standing on the front lawn with my purse hanging from my shoulder, I read. The article reported that a thirty-year-old man named Marc Malone had been arrested in his Royal Oak home on July 9. He was suspected of raping two women in the city of Ann Arbor in 1985, and local police detectives believed he was responsible for at least four other unsolved rapes in the cities of Berkley, Ferndale, and Oak Park during the first six months of 1987. It said nothing about Royal Oak. The article described a man who broke into women's houses in the early morning hours and used a nylon stocking to cover his face. He bound and gagged his victims and then raped them.

If this man was my assailant, he had, indeed, gone on to rape other women. Although it was possible that it wasn't the same man, it gave me hope that the capture of the man who attacked me was still a possibility. This was evidence that detectives continue to investigate crimes that happened months or even years previously. The newspaper also mentioned that a meeting had taken place between detectives from Royal Oak and the surrounding cities of Berkley, Oak Park, and Ferndale. A Royal Oak detective named Fred Earnshaw had remembered an incident with a peeping Tom from the previous year. Malone had been arrested, convicted of disorderly conduct, and sentenced to one year of probation. Detective Earnshaw sent a copy of Malone's fingerprints to the Michigan State Police where they were connected to several unsolved rape cases in Ann Arbor dating back to 1985. Evidence obtained after Malone's arrest for these rapes connected him to the assault in Berkley, a city that borders Royal Oak.

Ferndale and Oak Park were waiting for crime lab results to determine if Malone was the person responsible for rapes in their cities. Norm Raymond, a Ferndale detective, had put together a task force and organized a meeting of the Oakland County detectives. The newspaper praised the detectives who linked the rapes in the various cities. The Oak Park detective, Mary Timmons, was credited with originally contacting the Michigan State Police sex crimes unit in an effort to solve the crimes in her city.

Looking up from the paper, I noticed that my mother was staring at me intensely, waiting for my reaction. I was in total shock, since I had given up hope months ago of finding my attacker. When I finally spoke, I asked the obvious question. "Do you think the Royal Oak police will be calling me?"

"I would think so, although it probably wouldn't hurt to give them a call and remind them about your case," Mom urged. Looking at my watch, I noticed it was now after five o'clock.

Somewhat hesitant about calling Detective Shanahan in Royal Oak, I went in the house and looked up the number to the Berkley police station.

Detective Ray Anger was the name listed in the newspaper as the officer in charge of the Berkley case. Fortunately, he was still at the police station. Although he was polite to me, he told me that I would need to speak with a detective in Royal Oak.

"Darn it," I muttered under my breath as I hung up the phone. "I have no choice but to talk to Detective Shanahan again!"

It had been about six months since I had spoken with anyone from the Royal Oak police department, yet I still remembered the phone number. Dialing the phone, old feelings of apprehension came flooding back. *Will Detective Shanahan even remember me?* A male voice answered the phone. When I asked for Detective Elaine Shanahan, he said, "I'm sorry. Detective Shanahan left the department earlier this year. Would you like to leave a message with the detective who took her place?"

Detective Shanahan no longer works there! I gave him my name, phone number, and case number, then I hung up the phone.

Detective Fred Earnshaw called me the next day, Friday. He was a soft-spoken man with a casual manner who appeared eager to speak with me. The first time we would have the opportunity to meet in person would be Monday at five o'clock on my way home from work.

The weekend passed by slowly. Eager to speak to a different detective, I was hoping to finally find out if the man in custody could be my assailant. If I knew for sure that Malone was the right man, I believed that all of my fears would disappear.

When Monday finally came, I could barely contain my excitement, yet as I reached for the door handle of the Royal Oak police department, I hesitated. While attending the support group at HAVEN, I heard horror stories about women testifying in court against the person who raped them. They felt humiliated and re-victimized as they were forced to describe the details of the rapist's actions to a courtroom full of people. If I left now, maybe I could avoid these stressful court proceedings. The newspaper articles had mentioned that there were several police departments who would be charging him with assaults that occurred in their own communities. *Will one more really make a difference? Yet, if I don't talk to the police, I will never know for sure if the man I fear is off the streets.*

Taking a deep breath, I mustered up my courage and entered the building, in the hopes that I was entering a new, less fearful phase of my life. Inside, I reported to the lobby desk. A thick sheet of glass separated me from the man behind the counter. "I'm here to see Detective Earnshaw," I said in a nervous voice, louder than I needed to.

I was led to Detective Earnshaw's office, where I waited for him to appear. *What questions will he ask me? It has been almost one year since my assault. Will I be able to give him the detail he needs to determine if the man in custody is my assailant?*

During the assault, only the lower part of my attacker's face was visible when he lifted the stocking and exposed his mouth. The only other parts of his body I actually saw in my house were two fingers on his left hand. They were protruding from the white rubber gloves he was wearing. Surprisingly, the image of his two fingers was burned into my memory, and I believed I could identify them. But the image that I remembered most clearly was the one of him leaving my house and hurrying past my kitchen window. He had taken off the nylon stocking by this time. If given the opportunity to see him in person, I believed that I would know for sure if he was my attacker.

Finally, a man with sandy brown hair and glasses in his mid-thirties appeared and introduced himself as Detective Earnshaw. His smile was contagious, and I couldn't help but smile back. During our conversation, he spoke slowly and calmly, which put me at ease. He was easy to talk to, and I felt safe in his presence, just as I had with Ike McKinnon.

Our conversation focused on the similarities between my assault in Royal Oak and the assaults in Ann Arbor, Berkley, Oak Park, and Ferndale. Detective Earnshaw believed it was possible that the suspect they had in custody was also responsible for the assault against me! To help ensure that he would be ordered to stand trial in my case, forensic tests needed to be done on the samples collected from me during the rape kit at the hospital. Apparently, until they have a suspect, forensic tests are not run due to the enormous expense of doing them. They would compare the evidence gathered in the rape kit with the DNA of Marc Malone. Detective Earnshaw explained that recent advancements in this type of testing could determine whether it was likely that Malone was responsible for my assault. It had only been within the previous year that this testing had been made available to determine the guilt or innocence of suspected rapists and murderers during criminal trials.

Years later, I learned that in July 1987, no one in the United States had yet been convicted of a crime based on DNA testing. However, there had been several convictions in England. I was unaware of the tremendous impact this technology would have in crime reporting.

"When is the next time Marc Malone will appear in court?" I asked Detective Earnshaw.

"His preliminary examination is scheduled to be held in Berkley on August 4. The judge will be hearing testimony from both witnesses and law enforcement officials. He will determine if there is enough evidence for the case in Berkley to go to trial."

Although the thought of seeing the face of this suspected rapist was frightening, I wanted to attend the hearing. I said nothing to Detective Earnshaw.

I left the police station that day feeling confident, knowing that Detective Earnshaw would be the one handling the investigation and accompanying me during any potential legal proceedings. The amount of support I was receiving from male professionals surprised me. Sometimes, I think, people erroneously believe women are the most logical supporters for rape victims. I learned that a person's gender is not what determines the level of compassion of which he or she is capable.

Earnshaw, like many of my other new acquaintances, helped open my eyes to the goodness that existed in so many people. It was becoming easier to see God's signature on everything and everybody near me. I had not been abandoned.

It was five o'clock on the morning of Tuesday, August 4. Lying in bed with my eyes closed, I was hoping to fall back asleep for another hour or two before my alarm went off. My efforts were in vain. I couldn't relax knowing that I might soon be in the same room with the man who had wreaked havoc on my life. Yet, I was determined to see him and find out for sure whether the man the police had arrested was my assailant. Knowing that he would be physically restrained and unable to hurt anyone gave me the courage I needed to face him.

At six thirty I gave up trying to sleep and rolled out of bed. Several cups of tea later, my thoughts continued to dwell on the preliminary exam that would take place later that morning. *How long will the proceedings take? Will I need to explain my purpose for being there?* Suddenly, I noticed that Angel and Brandy were sitting at my feet staring at me. Preoccupied, I had forgotten to give our hungry pets their breakfast! Too nervous to eat anything myself, I showered early. At seven forty-five, I was ready to leave.

It was eight fifteen when I drove into the parking lot of the courthouse. In a few minutes Mom and her sister, my Aunt Marion, would arrive. Having never been in a courtroom before, I had no idea what to expect. *How large will the room be? How close will I be sitting to the man accused of these violent crimes? Should I hide myself in the back of the room so I won't be noticed, or should I bravely face the suspect from the front row?*

NINETEEN

A Moment of Truth

Mom's car pulled into the parking lot. Since court wouldn't begin for another forty-five minutes, I settled into her back seat. Deep in thought, I was anxious for the court proceedings to begin. As I fidgeted with the seat belt lying next to me, I tried to stop worrying. *What if he turns out to be the wrong man? Then what?*

Remembering his physical appearance was unsettling; however, I allowed myself to concentrate on the characteristics that I remembered most clearly: the color and texture of his hair, his profile as he walked past my window, his height, the rounded shape of his broad shoulders, and those two fingers that had been inches from my face. Perhaps I might even recognize the sound of his voice if given the chance to hear him speak. Whether he was guilty of the other assaults or not, I needed to know, without question, whether he was the one who broke into my house.

Looking down at my watch, I realized it was now eight forty-five. Mom, Aunt Marion, and I stepped out of the car. As we approached the courthouse, I read the words boldly printed on the glass door: "Berkley 45A District Court." Inside, a large crowd of people had gathered. Looking around, I observed that some were carrying large cameras and others held pencils and notebooks. Suddenly, it dawned on me that these people were journalists sent by television stations and newspapers to report about this accused serial rapist. It had never occurred to me that they would be such a large presence at this preliminary exam.

Nine o'clock came and went, and still we waited. Fortunately, I had taken the entire day off work, anticipating that it might take longer than I had expected. Finally, at nine thirty, we were allowed to enter the courtroom. One by one, we all squeezed through the doorway. Mom, Aunt Marion, and I were able to find a seat. I surveyed my surroundings. It was much different than I had expected, with the seating for spectators occupying only a small part of the space in the room. The judge's bench, witness stand, and additional seating for court officials were arranged in a horseshoe shape along the front and sides of the room. Two large tables facing the judge were positioned between the bench and the observers.

Suddenly, two men dressed in dark suits walked into the room, each of them taking a seat behind their respective tables. Both of them began busily shuffling through paperwork. My assumption was that they were attorneys. Each time someone new entered the courtroom, I studied their face in search of my assailant. So far, none of these strangers bore any resemblance to him or looked like a prisoner.

Aside from the door we had walked through, there was only one other entrance to the courtroom. It was located along the back wall, behind the judge's bench. My gaze darted back and forth between the two doors, wondering which entrance Marc Malone would be walking through. I noticed I was shivering. Folding my arms, I attempted to warm myself. *Is the air conditioning especially cold in this room? Or is anxiety causing me to tremble?*

Recognizing Malone as my attacker could have a tremendous impact on my psychological well-being. It could be the end of a life plagued by fear and paranoia. Even if I retained many of my current worries and suspicions, at least I would know that he was no longer watching me.

Although my primary concern was to stop my assailant from harming me or any future victim, I also wanted him punished! *I want him to feel the same pain that he inflicted on me when he ambushed me from Joanne's closet. I want him to know what it is like to believe that he is living his final moments on earth. I want him to be raped in prison in the same way that he raped me!*

As anger built up inside of me, I realized that I was reliving those terrifying moments again. Then, without notice, the figure of a man appeared in the doorway near the back of the courtroom! Wrists handcuffed in front of him, he was being led by a police officer.

Everything seemed to be moving in slow motion as he walked toward the seat beside the man sitting at one of the tables. I got a good look at his profile as he passed less than ten feet away from me! It was the same side I had observed as he escaped past my kitchen window. With the exception of the facial hair that now disguised his appearance, he had the same features that I had described to Officer Struble on the day of the rape. His shoulders were rounded, yet broad, beneath the blue-gray shirt that he was wearing. His cheeks were full, and he wore his dark-brown hair in a shorter style, although long enough to reveal a slight wave. Intuitively, I knew that this was the man who had caused all of my pain.

Initially the room became quiet, then the murmur of lowered voices began to spread throughout the courtroom. As Malone neared the seating where the onlookers were situated, he turned his head toward us and began studying individuals. My first instinct was to look away and hide behind the person in front of me, but with clenched teeth, I fought off that urge. Still trembling, I stared directly at him until our eyes finally met. At that moment, there was no doubt in my mind that not only did I recognize him, but that he also recognized me! I had not anticipated this encounter or his reaction. However, he had watched me for weeks before breaking into my house. Certainly he knew what I looked like, and probably even knew my name. The expression on his face was one of surprise and confusion as his dark eyes seemed to widen and stare. Since I was not one of his recent victims, he was probably surprised to see me in court.

Within me, I felt an eruption of tremendous strength and courage. No longer did I perceive my assailant as an indestructible monster who was free to terrorize me. Now he was a weak, pathetic human being who had been captured and restrained.

As my gaze shifted downward, I noticed that he carried a book into the courtroom. Looking closer, I could see the words "Holy Bible" written in gold letters on the front cover. *Did he suddenly find God after his arrest, or has he always carried a Bible around?* It troubled me that a person who was capable of causing so much suffering was now portraying himself as a Christian.

Appearing nervous, he took his seat next to his attorney and began talking to him quietly. Now I could only see the back of his head and his hunched shoulders, but I had seen enough. No longer able to look at this demon, I turned my head to the side. Now my only focus was to do whatever I could to make sure he went to prison. A feeling of hatred welled up within me, more than I had ever felt towards another human being. Leaning towards my mom, I angrily proclaimed, "It's him!"

Instantly, I noticed that she had the same clenched jaw, the same tight fists, and the same anger in her eyes that I had. It was the first time that I realized that her wounds were as deep, if not deeper, than mine. She looked as though she wanted to kill Malone, and was doing everything she could to restrain herself.

Fortunately, the tension was broken abruptly by a male voice loudly calling out, "All rise!" The judge had arrived. He sat down and began thumbing through the paperwork in front of him. Seconds later, the man seated at the opposite table from Malone stood up and began to speak. I assumed that he was the prosecutor.

"Calling the case of the People versus Marc Malone . . . Today is the time and date set for the preliminary exam in this matter. At this time, Your Honor, because of the nature of the charges in this case, the People would move pursuant to MCLA 966.9 that bystanders be excluded from the courtroom."

My mother and I turned toward each other, a look of confusion on our faces. The man sitting next to Malone then addressed the judge. He must have been the attorney for the defense. "We have discussed this matter with the prosecutor and the Court and we have no objections." The prosecuting attorney explained further: "This involves the removal of people who are not officers of the court or persons by law required to be in attendance at this matter."

The judge then spoke for the first time. "Pursuant to the statute and *Booth Newspapers v. Midland Circuit Court Judge,* the court will order the courtroom closed."

Everyone seated around us stood up and began walking out of the courtroom. Mom, Aunt Marion, and I followed, not completely understanding what was happening.

The hallway was even more crowded than before and I overheard many of the conversations. Apparently, the prosecuting attorney wanted the Berkley victim to testify without a room full of onlookers listening to the humiliating details of her attack. The people from the news media were calling their own attorneys in an effort to allow them back in the courtroom. Silently, I prayed that the reporters would lose this battle.

As I waited for the courtroom to reopen, I realized that there was no need for me to hear the rest of the preliminary exam. The victim's story would be the same as mine, and I already knew the ending. Mom and Aunt Marion followed me through the door and out to my car. Although they tried to talk me into going out for some lunch, I was in a hurry to get home and call Detective Earnshaw. My assailant had been captured after one long year of searching!

As soon as I got in the house, I called Detective Earnshaw. "He's the guy, detective. I'm sure of it!" I blurted out emphatically.

"Okay, Julie. Slow down. What do you mean?"

"I went to the Berkley preliminary exam for Marc Malone this morning. He passed right in front of me and I'm sure he's the same man that broke into my house."

"We need to take this one step at a time," Detective Earnshaw said calmly. "Do you know if they took any blood from you in the emergency room after the assault?"

"I don't remember." I replied.

"I'll give the crime lab a call, but it might take a day or so to get in touch with them. I'll let you know as soon as I hear anything."

Busying myself around the house, I waited for his call the remainder of the afternoon. Detective Earnshaw was extremely reliable. There was no doubt in my mind that he would call me the minute he heard from the crime lab. Yet, the longer I waited, the more uneasy I became. Now I wanted the opportunity to testify against my attacker. I wanted to confront him in court and let him know that he didn't destroy me or cause me to abandon my home. Knowing that he was now in a situation where he would be pleading for his own life and freedom helped me feel that I was the one in control.

TWENTY

THE EVIDENCE GROWS

The morning after the hearing, eager to know the outcome of the preliminary exam, I stopped in front of the local drugstore for a paper on the way to work. The headlines in the *Royal Oak Daily Tribune* were visible from the parking lot: "Judge Orders Malone to Stand Trial."

Leaning my head back against the car seat, I closed my eyes and breathed a sigh of relief. Apparently, the prosecution did a thorough job of presenting the evidence, yet in my mind, I credited the courage of the victim's testimony as the deciding factor.

During the past year, I had believed that I was kept in the dark about new developments in my case. Finally, the newspapers were providing me with the information that I was desperate to know. There was a direct correlation between the amount of knowledge I gained and the degree of control I felt in my life. I was grateful to the press in these early stages of the prosecution.

During the previous week, the media had reported that a potential "hit list" had been found in Malone's car with the names of eighty-three women, all Oakland County residents, along with their addresses, professions, and physical characteristics. Two of them were the daughters of police officers. The women ranged in age from sixteen to fifty, some of them still in high school. The discovery of the hit list had a chilling effect on the Oakland County community. A deluge of calls began pouring into the police stations—each woman wondering if her name was on "the list." It was not yet understood how the thirty-year-old suspect compiled the list of names or where he got his information. In remembering the weeks previous to my assault, I suspected that I might know the answer to that question. Several months before my house was broken into, I noticed some cassette tapes missing from my car. I wondered if it was Malone who had taken them, after rummaging through the glove box where I kept my car registration. Often I would leave work-related paperwork and material from my classes lying on the front seat. It would have been easy for him to find out my name and where I worked by looking at these items. Who knows how much information he might have been able to gather by looking in the cars and windows of these women!

After buying a copy of the newspaper, I went back to my car to read the latest article about the Berkley preliminary exam. Knowing that I had a full hour before the start of my shift at work, I took time to absorb the entire column.

The newspaper reported that there had been three hours of testimony, after which the judge ordered Malone to stand trial on a five-count felony warrant. It involved two counts of first-degree sexual assault, two counts of second-degree criminal sexual conduct, and one count of breaking and entering. Once again, the article mentioned that the police in Ferndale and Oak Park were seeking arrest warrants in connection with three additional sexual assaults. Malone was to remain in jail on bonds totaling two hundred thousand dollars.

The story also described the findings of testing done at the Michigan State Police Laboratory. An expert from this crime lab testified that DNA of the semen stains found on the victim's bed sheets matched Malone's blood type. The samples tested shared characteristics of the blood type in less than one percent of the population.

It was also discovered that the torn end on a roll of duct tape found in Malone's car matched the end of a piece of tape used to bind the victim. In his car, the police found a pair of sweatpants and a flashlight that was identified by the victim as hers.

Encouraged by the two-hundred-thousand-dollar bond that was set, I felt assured that Malone would stay in jail for the duration of the trial. There appeared to be a great deal of evidence mounting against him, and hopefully a guilty verdict would keep him locked away from society for a long time.

I began my drive to work. Although the sky was overcast, my spirits were high. Aware that most rapists were never apprehended at all, let alone prosecuted, I felt as though I was experiencing a miracle. The previous year had been a nightmare for me because my assailant had remained free, but I was beginning to understand that it was a far better thing that he was apprehended this year. DNA testing had become more widespread in 1987 than in 1986, and more physical evidence was available in the Berkley case than in my own. Apparently, God knows the appropriate time to answer our prayers. Sometimes the response may not be as immediate as we would like it to be, or in the exact manner that we expect, but I realized that how it comes is most likely in our best interest.

I was at work for less than five minutes when Detective Earnshaw called. He told me that no blood had been drawn from me at the hospital the morning of the rape, and that I would need to supply the crime lab with a sample of my own DNA in order for them to complete their tests. I agreed to meet him after work at a hospital in Royal Oak to have my blood drawn. The police department would ask them to rush these tests, but there were no guarantees as to when they would be complete. It could take weeks, possibly even months, before the results of the DNA analysis would be known.

In the days that followed the Berkley proceedings, Malone was arraigned on three additional assault cases. According to the *Daily Tribune,* he was arraigned on a ten-count warrant on August 6, charging him with the sexual assault of two Oak Park women earlier in 1987. The article mentioned that both of the women were assaulted during the night when an intruder broke into their homes. In each case, the assailant bound his victim, covered her face, and used some type of lotion during the sexual assault. While in the victim's homes, he wore a stocking covering his face and gloves on his hands. The newspaper article also described the ongoing investigation into the hit list they had found.

Throughout the next several weeks, many of the headlines focused on either the arraignments or preliminary exams of Marc Malone in connection with assaults in Oak Park, Ferndale, Berkley, or Ann Arbor. In each case the victim described an assault that was almost identical to my own. Each day I continued to stop for a copy of the newspaper on my way to work. Now that six other victims had been identified, I was feeling even more certain that Malone would not be released from jail.

It was during this time that I finally found the courage to be tested for the AIDS virus. When the test results were negative, it was an enormous relief. However, I still felt as though I was living in a kind of fog, unable to think as clearly as I would have liked or feel completely normal. *Maybe I will never get back to my old self.* I also began dating again.

On Friday, August 21, I was looking forward to the upcoming weekend. A coworker of mine, John, had asked me out on Saturday night. Then, on Sunday, I was invited to my parents' house for dinner to celebrate my twenty-seventh birthday.

John had asked if he could pick me up early on Saturday so he would have time to stop by the home of one of his friends before taking me to a Hank Williams Jr. concert. My family saw John as a ray of hope for their single daughter, maybe even a potential husband. My grandmother especially seemed worried that I might never get married. Sometimes I wondered if they thought I was damaged in some way because of the rape. Although I enjoyed John's company, he was not someone I would marry.

John picked me up in his Chevy, and within a few minutes we were on the expressway heading toward Pine Knob Music Theater. When he exited the expressway prematurely, I assumed he was taking me to his friend's house. He turned into a cluster of red-bricked apartment buildings, and I noticed several signs pointing us in the direction of the clubhouse. He parked his car in an empty spot near the front door.

"What are your friends doing in there?" I asked, pointing to the clubhouse.

"They are getting ready for a baby shower tomorrow. I just need to stop in and pick up a set of keys from them. Why don't you come in and meet them?"

Inside the clubhouse, it was dark. "Hey, John," I said, "I think your friends must have gone."

I never did hear his response.

TWENTY-ONE

ALIVE AGAIN!

Suddenly, the room lit up and I felt as though I had walked into a dream. The thunderous "SURPRISE!" that greeted me as I walked through the door sent a jolt, almost like an electric shock through every cell of my body. Familiar faces smiled at me from various places around the room. It took several seconds before I realized what was happening. This was a surprise birthday party for me!

Joanne, standing directly in front of me, opened her arms and gave me a tremendous hug. "Happy birthday, Jules!"

Still in shock, I somehow managed to stammer out a response. "Did you plan all of this, Jo?"

"Bernadette and I have been planning it for a while now," Joanne said smiling.

Bernadette was a dear friend who, like Joanne, I had known since the age of six. I couldn't imagine my life without them.

As I looked around the room, I saw friends and family from all different periods of my life. My old friend, Nancy, was at the party with her boyfriend. The close friendship we had shared before the rape was now a distant memory. Yet she came to my party and I was grateful.

Richard was there, along with Lisa and several others that I worked with at the Renaissance Center. These people were around me every day, and not one of them had said a word about this night. They had been a tremendous part of my support system during the previous year, going out of their way to help me through the most difficult times. Their presence on this evening reminded me of my many blessings.

My immediate family and Joanne's family came to celebrate with me, along with several of my old high school classmates.

Although the entire party lasted about four or five hours, it seemed to be over in a flash. Throughout the entire evening, I talked nonstop. All of my pent-up thoughts and emotions came spilling out of me. The opportunity to spend time with this group of about sixty dear friends and family gave me renewed energy and strength. Amazing things can happen when you feel loved!

When they yelled "surprise," I seemed to snap out of the stupor that I had been living in. A sudden, emotional jolt shot through me. I felt alive again!

While talking to Bernadette that evening, I told her how much I appreciated the party and about the impact that it had on me. I still remember her response: "It's funny that you should say that because planning the party was something that Joanne and I felt driven to do." *How could they have known that it was exactly what I needed?*

Near the end of September 1987, I received the phone call from Detective Earnshaw that I had been anticipating for almost two months.

"Julie, the results are back from the crime lab. We should have a date for Malone's arraignment any day now."

"An arraignment?" I hesitated for a moment, trying to remember exactly what that involved. "Does this mean that they found Malone's DNA in the evidence that was collected at the hospital?"

"They did what's called a serological comparison between your blood type, the samples collected at the hospital after the rape, and the blood obtained from Malone after he was caught. The semen found on your sweatpants and the vaginal swabs taken during your hospital exam match the DNA of only .08 percent of the general population. According to the test results, it definitely could have originated from Malone. Because of these findings, an arrest warrant will be issued first, and then a date will be set for his arraignment."

Finally, there was proof that Malone was my attacker! This meant that a court hearing in which Malone would be advised of the charges against him would happen soon. At that time he would be asked to plead guilty or not guilty and bond would be set by the judge. I would have an opportunity to speak out publicly. The thought of testifying in a court-room was terrifying, but I instinctively knew it was an important step in my recovery. This would be my chance to prove to Malone that my spirit had survived his attack!

Since I was naive about the criminal justice system, I decided it would be a good idea to educate myself. HAVEN was the best source of informa-tion that I could think of, so I contacted the advocacy office.

My phone call was returned by a woman named Judy who ran a one-woman department. Each time a victim of domestic violence or sexual assault needed assistance with the legal process, Judy helped educate her and accompanied her to court. She informed me that sitting on a witness stand was a stressful experience for almost everyone, including seasoned police officers. For the victim, facing the person you most fear makes it even more difficult. We agreed to meet later in the week at her office. Hopefully, this training would diminish some of the anxiety I was feeling about testifying.

When I walked into Judy's office for the first time, I looked around in amazement at the amount of paperwork she had on her desk and around her office. Stacks of newspaper and magazine articles were stored on shelves. Small pieces of paper with hand-written notes covered her work-space. Before our conversation began, the phone rang several times and it became clear that her job pulled her in many directions. Although I might have expected her to rush through our conversation, she did just the oppo-site. Her calm and gentle demeanor made it easy to talk to her, and she gave me her full attention; her kind, brown eyes never shifting their attention from mine. She was informative, patient, and easy to understand. In less than an hour, I gained significant knowledge of the criminal justice system. That knowledge empowered me with courage and self-confidence.

Two days later, the words on the front page of the October 3 edition of the *Royal Oak Daily Tribune* startled me at first glance: "Malone Named in '86 Rape." Even though I knew about the arrest warrant in connection with my own case, it was still a shock to see it in print. My cries had finally been heard.

Malone was being charged with two counts of first-degree criminal sexual conduct, two counts of second-degree sexual conduct, and one count of breaking and entering. His arraignment was scheduled for Monday, October 5, 1987. The article detailed the date of my sexual assault, but did not name me or give any further information. It stated that recently completed laboratory tests linked Malone to my rape. There was no turning back now. The legal process was in motion, and it appeared that my day in court was quickly approaching.

Detective Earnshaw informed me that I was not required to attend the arraignment on Monday. That was good news, since getting time off from my job was difficult. I was sure that he would let me know if anything unexpected were to happen. The morning of the arraignment, I went to work as usual, but my mind was on what was happening in that courtroom.

Detective Earnshaw called me early that afternoon. "Just thought I'd let you know the preliminary exam is scheduled for October 16, less than two weeks away. You will be called as a witness to testify."

"I'll be ready," I told him, with a confidence that surprised even me.

A short article describing Malone's arraignment appeared in the *Daily Tribune* the following day. My eyes grew wide as I read his bold request, made after the charges were read. Malone had asked the judge to set a low bond so he "wouldn't be placed with overly violent people" in the Oakland County jail! What brazen denial! Apparently, he didn't consider shoving, binding, gagging, and raping a woman to be a violent act. Surely, he would rape again if given the chance! The judge had denied his request, and set bail at one hundred thousand dollars.

During the following two weeks, I spoke with either Detective Earnshaw or Judy each time I began to feel nervous or apprehensive. They answered all of my questions with amazing patience. *Will he be in the courtroom while I testify? Do I need to look at him? Will Malone have the opportunity to speak?*

My family and friends were also a tremendous support to me during those nerve-wracking days preceding the preliminary exam. Although I didn't tell them how terrified I was of sitting on the witness stand, I sensed that many of them knew and were praying for me as October 16 approached.

For over a year, I had wondered if the capture of my rapist would make a difference in my life and my recovery. Now the man I feared above all others was being held securely behind the bars of a prison cell. A tremendous burden had been lifted. I had the reassurance that I wasn't being stalked. Still, it wasn't quite the drastic improvement that I had expected. I felt safer, but there seemed to be no magic solution to getting rid of all the emotional and psychological affects of the rape.

The subpoena ordered me to appear at Royal Oak's Forty-Fourth District Court at nine o'clock on Friday, October 16, 1987. Surprisingly, I was considered a witness for this trial, the plaintiff being the People of the State of Michigan. It seemed odd to label the victims of crimes as witnesses, as if they had watched the assault from a distance.

The date arrived quickly, and the angst that I felt the morning of the preliminary exam is almost beyond description. Although I know that I drove myself to the courthouse that day, I have little memory of getting ready that morning or of the two-mile drive to downtown Royal Oak. My mom was waiting for me just inside of the courthouse entrance. We had been instructed to meet the prosecuting attorney in the hallway outside of Judge Daniel Sawicki's courtroom on the third floor. If Mom said anything to me as we walked up the three flights of stairs, I was too preoccupied to hear her. Staring at the light-green tiles that lined the bottom half of the wall in this old Royal Oak building, I took deep breaths in an attempt to calm my nerves.

Exhausted from a restless night and constant worry, I was unable to get rid of the headache I woke up with, while a queasy stomach had made it impossible to eat breakfast. Each time I opened a door or brushed the hair from my face, I noticed my hand trembling.

As we reached the landing on the top floor, Detective Earnshaw was there and introduced us to Brian Zubel, the attorney for the prosecution.

We all went into the waiting room next to the courtroom and sat down around a table. My mother, Detective Earnshaw, and myself remained quiet as Brian Zubel talked about the hearing that was about to get underway. He explained that the preliminary trial would not determine the defendant's guilt or innocence. Its function was to provide an opportunity for the prosecution to present the evidence before a judge. If the facts were convincing, the case would be bound over to circuit court. From my meeting with Judy, I already knew that the preliminary exam takes place in the district court of the city where the crime occurred. If bound over to circuit court, the defendant is then tried by a jury, or by a judge without a jury, at the Oakland County Courthouse in Pontiac, Michigan.

Brian then explained that the attorney for the defense was a man named Jacob Larkins. He would do everything in his power to discredit the evidence and my testimony. Upon entering the room, I should sit next to the judge in the witness stand. After being sworn in, Brian would be the first one to question me about what had happened during the days that preceded the rape and also the morning of the assault. Brian asked if I wanted the courtroom closed to reporters and other observers in the same way it had been done in Berkley. Without hesitation, I agreed, believing it would be easier to testify in front of fewer people. Knowing that it was necessary to give a detailed account of what had happened during the assault, I was extremely anxious about using all of the appropriate sexual terms and pronouncing them correctly. The words *labia* and *cunnilingus* were not part of my usual vocabulary. I had seen these words in print more often than I had heard them pronounced.

Although my mom had stayed by my side throughout the past year, I wasn't comfortable having her in the courtroom during my testimony. The anger she felt towards Malone was extreme. There was a part of me that was afraid of how she might react when put in the same room with the man who had hurt me.

About five minutes into Brian's instruction, Judy from HAVEN appeared in the doorway. Quietly, she slid into the waiting room and found an empty seat at the table. Glancing around the room, I was reminded that I had been blessed with a special group of people to help me through this ordeal. Within each of these professionals, there existed a compassionate nature that extended far beyond the job they were being paid to do. I knew that it was more than just luck that had brought Detective Earnshaw, Judy, and Brian Zubel into my life.

Brian prepared me for what to expect during the hearing. He did almost all of the talking, and made several suggestions in regards to my testimony. "It is important, Julie, that you listen carefully to the questions and don't let anyone rush you," he warned.

"What if I don't know the answer to a question?" I asked nervously.

"Then you need to convey that to the court," Brian replied. "Always tell the truth. Malone's attorney might try to mislead you with the way he phrases his questions. Make sure that you understand what he's asking before you give your answer." At the time I thought I would be grateful if I could just make it through the hearing without passing out. *Can I calmly answer the questions of the lawyer who is trying to free Malone?*

It was now nine thirty and the hearing was scheduled to begin at ten o'clock. With each minute that passed, I became more nervous. Yet, in spite of my fears, I was determined to face this monster and be as strong as possible in front of him. I was tired of feeling like a coward!

At nine forty-five, Mom, Judy, and I were the only ones left in the room. Both of them continued to encourage me as the minutes slowly passed. Judy had this amazing ability to convince me that I was capable of anything. Her confidence in me helped me to believe in myself. My mom had been my constant emotional support throughout the previous year. The strength by which she has always handled difficult situations inspired me to do the same.

Ten o'clock came and went. It was unsettling to be kept in the dark about what was happening in the courtroom and not know when I would be called. The tension in my neck and shoulders was growing, and I was worried that my headache would become unbearable.

Waiting made me so nervous that I could barely hold a conversation with Mom or Judy. *How will I be able to speak on the witness stand?* My entire body was trembling. *In this condition, will I even be able to walk into the courtroom?*

The idea of being in the same room with Malone again troubled me more than anything else. I had been told that I would only need to look at him one time; however, the thought of doing even that terrified me. I would be asked to point him out and identify him as the man who broke into my house. The rest of the time I could look directly at the attorney who was questioning me. Knowing that Detective Earnshaw would be in the courtroom the entire time would be a great source of strength.

The click of the door latch opening interrupted my thoughts. When I looked up, Detective Earnshaw was standing in the doorway looking directly at me. "They're ready for you now," he said, in the calm, gentle voice that I had grown accustomed to. Slowly, I stood up and walked through the door. Swallowing hard, I made an attempt to calm my nerves and settle my stomach. It didn't work.

TWENTY-TWO

MY TURN

Continuing to walk the twelve or so feet to the door of the court-room, I braced myself for the questioning that I would face. Although I was aware of the many bystanders lingering in the hallway, I focused my sight on the floor tiles, avoiding their stares. Upon reaching the door to the courtroom, I stopped, lifted my head, and looked directly into the familiar blue eyes of the detective. Although I can't quite explain it, Detective Earnshaw had a way of calming the storm within me. From deep within his eyes, I received the confidence that I needed to keep my composure under those stressful conditions.

Slowly, I took my first step into the courtroom. Hesitating for just a second, I looked only at the judge's bench, avoiding the rest of the room. Detective Earnshaw leaned toward me and whispered, "Take your seat on the witness stand to the right of Judge Sawicki."

Terrified at the thought of sitting at the front of the room, next to the judge, I forced myself to continue walking toward him. Sensing his eyes on me, I instinctively looked in Judge Sawicki's direction. Although I expected him to be intimidating, he wasn't. Smiling at me, he nodded his head in a welcoming gesture. Suddenly, I wanted to sit next to this judge whom I had been afraid of moments earlier.

From the corner of my eye, I could see several people sitting at tables directly in front of the judge, toward the center of the courtroom. Assuming that the defense attorney and Marc Malone were among these men, I refused to look in their direction. Instead, I focused on Detective Earnshaw who was now standing in the back of the courtroom. Since the judge had ordered the courtroom closed during my testimony, there were no spectators or press.

When Brian Zubel began his questioning, I looked only at him; I tried to pretend that we were the only people in the courtroom. "Ma'am, if you would state your name for the record."

"Julie Frawley."

"And would you spell your last name please?" Brian continued.

"F-R-A-W-L-E-Y."

"And ma'am, do you live in the city of Royal Oak?"

"Yes, I do."

Grateful for these initial basic questions, I was able to relax slightly. The prosecutor continued his questioning. "Were you living there back on August 29 of last year?"

"Yes, I was."

"And prior to that, say, in the prior week or two weeks, did you become suspicious or concerned for your safety while living at that address?"

"Yes, I was," I responded, and described the disturbing phone call I had received in the early morning hours, weeks before the assault. My heart began beating faster, anticipating the next question.

Brian continued. "And directing your attention to August 29, when you got up, what happened?"

Taking a deep breath, I was forced to think back to the morning of the assault. So far, I had remained strong, but now I had to relive the morning of the rape, with my assailant listening to my every word! Since I had described the details of that terrifying morning on at least five other occasions, I had learned to tell it without actually feeling the terror and emotions that accompanied the actual rape. I worried that in my testimony, the horrible trauma of the rape would be masked by my stubborn refusal to show my emotions and fear. *Will the severity and authenticity of the crime committed against me be questioned if I remain calm? Will it make me less believable?* What mattered most to me was that my pain was hidden from Malone. Detail by detail, I described every minute of the assault without shedding a single tear!

Although difficult, this opportunity to testify turned out to be a blessing in that I was able to take back a part of my spirit that he had savagely stolen from me that August morning. I wanted him to be afraid. Throughout the entire forty-five minutes that I was on the witness stand, I felt confident in my testimony. My memory of that morning's events was strong and lucid, and I did not waiver in my description of Malone's actions.

Near the end of the questioning by the prosecution, Brian Zubel began asking about the appearance of my attacker. So far, I had been able to avoid looking at Malone in the courtroom, although I knew the time was coming where I would be forced to see his face. "Did you go anywhere where you saw the person that you feel did these things to you?" asked Brian Zubel.

"After that day?" I asked, confused by the question.

"Yes."

"I went to the preliminary exam in Berkley," I answered.

"Was that at the request or at the suggestion of any police officer or prosecutor?"

"No, sir. I read about it in the paper, and I wanted to see him."

"And you just decided to go? Okay. And when you went down there, did you see a person that you believe was the same person who attacked you?"

"Yes, sir."

"All right. Is that person here in court today?"

"Yes, he is."

"Would you point him out and identify him for the court?"

These were the words I was dreading. *If I can just get past this part I will be okay.* The thought of our eyes meeting like they did in the Berkley courtroom was more than I believed I could handle.

Slowly, I turned my head to the right. Looking beyond Brian Zubel, I allowed myself to survey the rest of the courtroom. I looked at the rectangular table in the center of the room. Although I was trembling, I was in a hurry to be done with this identification process. I looked closely at the people behind the table and held my breath.

Unfortunately, both Malone and his attorney were looking directly at me. The face of my assailant was completely expressionless. A shiver ran through my body and I tried to look through him instead of dwelling on his face, but it was impossible. Once again, my eyes met Malone's, and I was overwhelmed with disgust. "He's sitting over there!" I blurted out, pointing towards the table. "He has a light-blue shirt on, dark-brown hair." Quickly I looked away, returning my focus to the prosecutor.

Brian Zubel turned toward Judge Sawicki and spoke. "Your Honor, may the record reflect identification of the defendant."

Although relieved that the identification was done, I knew that the more difficult questions were yet to come. The attorney for the defense would now have the opportunity to question me.

The first time I really got a good look at Jacob Larkins was when he approached the witness stand after Brian Zubel sat down. He was an older man with graying hair and short in stature. Throughout most of the time that he questioned me, his primary concern seemed to be the condition of my eyesight. Since I wasn't wearing my contact lenses the morning of the rape, he persisted in questioning me about how well I was able to see my assailant. "On this day in question, did you have your contacts in place?" Mr. Larkins asked.

"No." I answered simply.

"And you say that this man walked by within ten feet or so of you?"

"After he left the house, yes," I responded.

"And how long would you say it was from the time this incident started until you were talking to the police?" Mr. Larkins asked.

"Forty-five minutes."

"Do you recall giving the police a statement?"

"Yes."

He proceeded to ask me numerous questions about when I gave the statement and who wrote it out. His next question shocked me. "Do you recall telling the police officer that you weren't wearing your contact lenses, so you were unable to tell if the subject was even wearing a stocking over his head or not?"

"I did not say that!" I shot back. It felt as though I was being baited.

Now I knew what Brian meant when he told me to listen carefully to the questions I was being asked. He was twisting the words in my original statement to the police to make it look as though I was incapable of identifying my attacker. It suddenly felt as though I was the one on trial!

Many of his questions seemed to focus on my conversations with police officers and whether or not it was at their suggestion that I went to the Berkley preliminary exam. He spent a great deal of time asking me whether my request for the police records on this case was done on my own or whether it was at the suggestion of the Royal Oak police department.

His questions made me more and more angry. Yet, instead of feeling humiliated or embarrassed, I began to feel stronger and more self-assured. Certain that the right man was in custody, I would not allow Mr. Larkins to portray me as a befuddled victim.

When his questioning was done, the judge asked me to return to the waiting room outside of the courtroom. As I walked past the crowd of reporters and other observers in the hallway, I held my head high, feeling as though I had won this round. It was then that I remembered what I learned in my support group.

The counselors at HAVEN were adamant about referring to victims of rape and domestic violence as *survivors*. It was their belief that women who had experienced abuse could draw strength from the manner in which they labeled themselves. A *victim* is someone who sees herself as being alone and vulnerable, often dwelling on her own suffering. *Victims*, still gripped by the power of the crime committed against them, see no way of escaping their fear and sadness. This, unfortunately, was an accurate description of how I felt during the months following the assault. *How could I call myself a survivor when I needed to rely on others for a sense of peace and security?*

Survivors are hopeful that one day they will regain their confidence and strength, and they are beginning to see glimpses of that happening. Thinking of myself as a survivor didn't mean that I wasn't affected by the sexual assault or that it was no longer on my mind. It did mean that I would never give up the fight to achieve the peaceful existence that I longed for. Although there were many incidents that assisted in my transition from victim to survivor, a definite turning point occurred that day during the Royal Oak preliminary exam. Previously, I couldn't shake the feeling that my assailant had stolen a part of my spirit when he fled from my home. I struggled to understand exactly what was missing and how to get it back. Without this part of my spirit, I was unable to smile, experience happiness, and confront my fears. During my testimony, a missing part of my spirit reemerged. I realized that now my fears could no longer paralyze me. I believed that tomorrow could be better than today.

Throughout my experience, I had been continually aware of God's presence in the compassionate people who surrounded me. Now, I was beginning to understand that His answers to my prayers could also be found within me.

The tears that I cried when I returned to the waiting room were tears of joy.

On the day that followed the Royal Oak preliminary exam, it was reported that Malone was ordered to stand trial on six felony charges resulting from the August 29, 1986 break-in. As a result of my testimony, two additional first-degree offenses were now included in the charges. There were now four first-degree charges, one second-degree charge, and one charge of breaking and entering. In rape cases, the sexual acts committed by the perpetrator are classified as either first-, second-, third-, or fourth-degree offenses. First- and third-degree acts involve sexual penetration. According to the Michigan Criminal Sexual Conduct Act, penetration is the "entry into a person's genital opening or anal opening by the defendant's penis or finger or tongue or object. Any entry, no matter how slight, is enough." It can also be the "entry into a person's mouth by the defendant's penis," the "touching of a person's genital openings or genital organs with the defendant's mouth or tongue," or the "entry by any part of one person's body or some object into the genital or anal opening of another person's body." The main difference between first- and third-degree charges is usually determined by the person's age or whether or not there was personal injury.

Second- and fourth-degree offenses involve sexual contact with sexual purpose. The Michigan Criminal Sexual Conduct Act describes sexual contact as including "the intentional touching of the victim's or actor's intimate parts or the intentional touching of the clothing covering the immediate area of the victim's or actor's intimate parts, if that intentional touching can reasonably be construed as being for the purpose of sexual arousal or gratification, done for a sexual purpose, or in a sexual manner for revenge, to inflict humiliation, or out of anger." The term "actor" is used to describe the perpetrator. The difference between second- and fourth-degree charges is also usually determined by the person's age or whether or not there was personal injury.

The trial date was set for February 8, 1988. The prosecutor's office had decided there would be one trial in Oakland County during which the court would hear testimony from each of the five victims. There would be a separate trial in Washtenaw County for the cases involving the two Ann Arbor women. Since Brian Zubel was busy with several other cases, Attorney Lyle Kaplan was given the task of preparing the five Oakland County women for the trial. In order to make sure that we knew what was expected of us, we met individually with Mr. Kaplan the week before the trial of Marc Malone. Although Brian was unable to attend this meeting, Judy from HAVEN remained by my side.

While waiting to speak with Mr. Kaplan, I noticed another woman also waiting. As I sat there deciding whether or not to approach her, she walked in my direction. She smiled and introduced herself to me as one of the Oak Park witnesses. I immediately took comfort in her presence. Although our conversation was brief, she mentioned some of the devastating effects that the rape had had on her life. A feeling of sadness lingered within me after we talked. If Malone had been caught immediately following my assault, she would have been spared her terrifying ordeal.

Her knowledge of the court system seemed greater than my own, and she spoke out defiantly against the injustices that she had experienced thus far. The court was originally going to make each of Malone's five Oakland

County victims testify at five different trials. This woman fought to have one trial where each of us would be called to the witness stand once. It was reassuring to know that she was protecting all of us when she had challenged the criminal justice process.

The woman from Oak Park spoke highly of the detective who was assigned to both Oak Park cases. Her name was Mary Timmons, and I would soon learn that the two victims in her city had the same amount of respect for her as I had for Fred Earnshaw, the Royal Oak detective. Detective Timmons was described as a caring woman who was devoted to her job. Apparently, compassion and dedication are common traits among many detectives.

After a twenty-minute wait, I was called in to speak with Lyle Kaplan. This attorney was all business. I found it difficult to talk to him. His method of questioning was even more demeaning than that of Malone's defense attorney at the preliminary trial. While describing the details of my assault yet again, I was berated and made to feel like an immature child. Apparently, the phrase "between my legs" did not provide the detail or impact Mr. Kaplan was looking for. "How old are you anyway?" he snapped. Before I could answer him, he shot back, "You sound like a ten year old! Speak like an adult!" By the scowl on his face I could tell that he was thoroughly disappointed in me.

Every part of me wanted to break down crying and run out the door. Biting my lower lip, I steadied my emotions and continued speaking. I told myself that however embarrassing this was, it might help prepare me for the trial. Still, that didn't diminish the hostility I felt towards him at that moment. No wonder so many women decide not to report being raped! My appreciation for Brian Zubel's softer approach grew. When Brian spoke to me, my confidence soared. My interaction with Lyle Kaplan left me feeling as though I was a poor witness. Without question, this meeting turned out to be the most humiliating of all my experiences with the criminal justice system.

The subpoena commanded me to appear at the Pontiac courthouse at eight thirty a.m. on February 8. Driving down Telegraph Road, I blamed my uncontrollable shivering on the frigid outdoor temperatures. It was more likely the result of my inner turmoil. In spite of my fears, I knew that I would be able to testify. I was determined to help get Malone off the streets.

My understanding was that each of the five Oakland County victims would be present in court, along with the detectives in charge of their cases. Detective Earnshaw had told me that I would be the first witness to testify. Although this information made me more stressed, I was relieved that it would be over quickly. *Surely I can do this just one more time.*

TWENTY-THREE

TESTIMONY SILENCED!

The courthouse was easy to spot and my mom was waiting for me at the door. We had been told to meet with Brian Zubel outside of Judge Norman Lippitt's courtroom at eight o'clock. As we walked down the long hall to the courtroom, we saw Detective Earnshaw and a woman, who I assumed to be the Oak Park detective. A few reporters that I had noticed in attendance at the Berkley preliminary trial were also mingling nearby.

Detecive Earnshaw greeted us, a friendly smile on his face. "Good morning, ladies," he said warmly.

I smiled and nodded, grateful for his peaceful presence.

Trying not to stare, I began looking around at the crowd that surrounded me, hoping to see Malone's other victims. With the exception of the Oak Park woman I had seen in Lyle Kaplan's office, I was unsure if I would even recognize them.

Within the next five minutes, more people began arriving, including Judy from HAVEN. Now I felt certain that I was not the only victim present. In addition to the woman I had met outside of Lyle Kaplan's office, Detective Anger from Berkley was talking with a small group of people, although none of them appeared young enough to be the Berkley victim. In remembering the preliminary trial in that city, I wasn't sure if I ever really saw her, although I knew she was twenty years old. Since I had never met Detective Raymond from Ferndale, I wasn't sure if he or the victim from that city were present.

Finally, I saw Brian Zubel approaching the growing crowd of people waiting outside of Judge Lippit's courtroom. The expression on his face was serious, although I noticed a slight smile forming on his lips. He motioned for me and several of the other women to approach him. Brian spoke slowly and calmly, as if to make certain that we would all understand what he was telling us.

"Malone has decided to plead guilty to criminal sexual assault in each one of the cases." Although his words were clear, it took several seconds for their meaning to sink in. *Does this mean there will be no trial?* Everyone was silent for what seemed like an eternity. Finally, one of the women asked the question that was on all of our minds. "Does this mean that we will not be called to testify?"

Brian responded, "That's correct. None of you will be called to the witness stand." He was now smiling broadly, and I felt like I should be smiling, too. Relief and disappointment flooded through me at the same time. While I was thrilled that we would not have to testify against Malone, a part of me felt robbed of the opportunity to speak out once again and make the devastating effects of this crime known to everyone within earshot.

Brian continued speaking. "Malone claims that he is pleading guilty to spare his victims the agony and humiliation of testifying on the witness stand." I found that statement hard to believe. Knowing the viciousness that he was capable of, I couldn't imagine that he was concerned about anyone other than himself.

Most of the people around me were smiling, and a few were hugging each other. Now I was better able to figure out which of these women were his victims; however, I only counted four of us. The others seemed relieved that they would avoid reliving their nightmare. *Does Malone believe that the evidence against him is overwhelming? Maybe he doesn't want to experience the embarrassment of hearing us tell a courtroom full of people what he has done to us.*

Mom's expression had changed from worry to one of great joy. The man who had hurt her daughter would now be punished. Knowing she was relieved gave me some degree of comfort.

"We are still trying to work out a few details," Brian continued. "I'll let you know when we are ready." He disappeared down the hallway as quickly as he had appeared.

During the next forty-five minutes, we all stood in that hallway nervously waiting to enter the courtroom. There was no way he was going to escape prison time now. He had admitted that he committed these horrible crimes, and hopefully no judge would allow him to be free to rape again. As we all stood in that hallway, questions raced through my mind. *What are the details of the plea agreement? Will Malone receive fewer years in prison because of it? Will we have an opportunity to tell Malone exactly what we think of him?*

My thoughts were interrupted by the sound of Judy's voice. She said that when a person pleads guilty to a crime, the prosecutors usually agree to dismiss one or more of the pending charges against him. This was a troublesome thought, and I wondered how it would affect his sentence. I remembered hearing that the crime of rape was not always taken seriously, and that rapists were sometimes known to receive lenient sentences.

At about nine fifteen, Brian Zubel returned to the crowded corridor and announced, "We will be dismissing all but the most serious charge for each case. Five charges will remain, and twenty-one others will be dismissed. This means that he will be sentenced based on four first-degree charges and one second-degree charge. His sentencing will not occur, though, until later in the month." Brian must have noticed the worried look on several of our faces because he quickly added, "It should be a long time before he is released." The crowd seemed to breathe a collective sigh of relief. Brian went on. "All of you are welcome to come into the room and listen to the terms of the plea agreement if you like. We should be starting in just a few moments." He opened the door to the courtroom. We all walked in after him.

Shortly before nine thirty, Malone was brought in wearing handcuffs and was seated on the opposite side of the room from where I was sitting. He showed no emotion whatsoever, and he completely avoided eye contact with anyone in the courtroom. He looked tired and worn.

Brian Zubel was the first one to speak. "Your Honor, recalling the matters of the People versus Marc Malone."

Malone's attorney was next. "Jacob P. Larkins, appearing for and on behalf of the respondent."

It was Brian's turn again. "Your Honor, we have entered into a plea agreement in these matters and if the court will indulge me for a few minutes, I think I can state it for the record. With regard to [case number] Your Honor, the defendant is charged with a total of six counts. He will plead guilty to first-degree criminal sexual conduct, that being count one."

He was talking about my case now. Five of the counts against him were being dismissed. Therefore, he was pleading guilty to only the most serious of his offenses.

During the next five minutes we listened to Brian read the case numbers of each of Malone's Oakland County victims and specify the counts to which he was pleading guilty. When he was finished, he looked up from the papers he was holding, faced Judge Lippitt, then continued speaking. "In all of these matters, there are additional counts, Your Honor. Should the court accept the pleas of guilty as already delineated, that being four counts of criminal sexual conduct in the first degree, one count of criminal sexual conduct in the second degree, those being the primary counts in each of the five files pending against this defendant, the People would move to dismiss the companion charges or the supplemental charges in each case." He then named each case once again and listed the counts being dismissed.

Judge Lippitt turned towards Jacob Larkins, Malone's attorney. "All right, Mr. Larkins. Do you see any reason why I can't question Mr. Malone on the voluntariness of the pleas on all of them at once?"

"No, Your Honor, your reputation of getting down to the facts—"

Judge Lippitt interrupted. "All right. Mr. Malone, did you hear the recitation by the prosecutor's office by Mr. Zubel?"

"Yes, Your Honor," he mumbled. For the first time since he had been in my living room, I heard Marc Malone's voice. I shivered.

The judge continued questioning Malone, making absolutely certain that he understood the charges against him and that he was not being pressured into pleading guilty. "All right. Has Mr. Larkins read and explained to you the charges set forth in each of the informations that have been filed against you?"

"Yes, he has, Your Honor," Malone answered.

"Is this plea the result of a plea bargain between yourself, Mr. Larkins, and the prosecuting attorney?" Judge Lippitt asked.

"That's what I understand, Your Honor, yes."

"Do you know the maximum sentence for these offenses is life in jail?" the judge continued.

"Yes." Malone's response was barely audible.

Once again, Judge Lippitt continued with his questioning, verifying that Malone understood that he had the right to a trial by jury in each case.

"Do you understand that when I accept your pleas of guilty, you will not have a trial of any kind, you give up all the rights which I've just explained to you, if you went to trial?"

"Yes, sir, I understand that," was Malone's monotone response.

After the judge was convinced that Malone was not threatened or coerced in any way into pleading guilty, he began questioning Malone about each individual case. Once again, I recognized the case number of the first case referenced as my own.

"The first one I have before me is [case number], and according to the plea form that you have signed . . . you signed the plea form?" the judge suddenly questioned.

"Yes, I did this morning, Your Honor," Malone answered.

"All right. This offense took place in Royal Oak, is that true?" the judge continued.

"I'm familiar with that case, yes, Your Honor." I could feel my shoulders stiffen.

"All right. And I understand the complainant in this case is someone by the name of Julie Frawley . . . F-R-A-W-L-E-Y?" The judge was having trouble pronouncing my last name.

"Yes, Your Honor," Malone responded.

"Okay," continued Judge Lippitt. "What, if anything did you do in that case, that causes you to believe that you're guilty of criminal sexual conduct in the first degree?" Closing my eyes tightly, I held my breath and braced myself for his response.

"I conducted sexual relations with Julie Frawley against her will."

"Where?"

"In her home," Malone answered.

His words made me cringe. What happened in my living room that morning was nothing like "sexual relations." Judge Lippitt continued with his questioning. "Okay. These sexual relations, did they involve penetration?" the judge asked.

"Yes, Your Honor, they did."

As difficult as it was to hear those words, I was glad that I was present when Malone admitted it publicly. When I had first heard that Malone intended to plead guilty, a part of me was disappointed that the public would not get a chance to hear about the evil that this man was capable of. At the time, I wanted his friends and family to know that this was not the man they thought he was. Most of all, I wanted the court to know that he was a dangerous man that should never be freed. Yet, the more I thought about it, the more I was satisfied with the plea bargain. Hopefully, there would be no chance of anything going wrong now.

Judge Lippitt continued questioning Malone as to his involvement in the other four cases. The entire process was completed very quickly, taking less than fifteen minutes. When it was over, a sentencing date of March 21 was set.

I was disappointed that it would be another month and a half before I would find out how long a sentence Malone would receive. Admittedly, I was eager to see the expression on his face as he was led off to prison. At the time I believed that seeing Malone suffer would give me great pleasure.

TWENTY-FOUR

MAKING A DIFFERENCE

As the sentencing of Marc Malone drew near, reporters for local television stations and newspapers wanted to give the public more information about his crimes and victims. HAVEN was often contacted with requests for information. Through HAVEN, reporters called me several times to ask for interviews. Since it is the policy of the newspapers not to use the real names of rape victims in their stories, I was given a fictitious name for each interview. They would offer to disguise my appearance for this type of story, although I didn't mind it if people that knew me recognized me. My only concern was to keep my real name out of the news to prevent other predators from finding me.

Often, I was asked if I felt used or exploited by these reporters. Certainly, I recognized that their main goal was to write a story that would sell papers. Still, I wanted to warn other women that this can really happen to them and they need to be aware of their surroundings. I also wanted to take the secrecy and the shame out of the crime of rape. If I wasn't afraid to talk about it, maybe other women would lose their fear of speaking out. I believed then, as I do now, that the silence that usually follows a rape makes it easier for sexual predators to get away with their crimes.

There were consequences from speaking to these reporters. I learned that there were no guarantees that the quotes that I felt were most important would be used in their stories. They often focused more on the perpetrator than the victim. On one occasion, Malone and I were interviewed separately for a story being written by one of the largest newspapers in the Detroit area. Although I had been told that this reporter would be interviewing Malone for the story, I was assured that they would not put our articles side by side as though it was a "him versus her" issue. However, that was exactly what they did. The article was titled "Interview with a Rapist", suggesting that Malone had a sort of celebrity status and had been the only one interviewed. Although I didn't regret the interview, I learned to use caution when talking with reporters. It seemed like a powerful way to share an important message with a large number of people. Unfortunately, the media has control over how that message is delivered.

During this time period, I no longer needed the emotional security of a rape support group, yet I still felt drawn to HAVEN. Grateful for all that they had done for me, I wondered if I could help other women who were left traumatized by violent acts committed against them. Judy suggested that I enroll in the volunteer courses at HAVEN, and I took her advice.

After several weeks of training, my first assignment was to answer HAVEN's crisis line. My job was to give information to people calling with questions about domestic violence and sexual assault. For a brief time, I volunteered in a program that involved responding to women who were recent victims of rape. I listened to their concerns, let them know someone cared, and gave them information about how to find the help they needed.

My life was beginning to improve and I was feeling more productive. In January 1988 I interviewed for a new position within my company and was given the job. It was located closer to home with regular working hours. It was at this new building that I met an interesting young man named Chris, and we began dating. Finally the intense loneliness was fading.

After Malone's plea, Brian Zubel told us that each of Malone's victims would be given the chance to speak out at the sentencing about the effect the crime had on their own lives. The purpose of this victim impact statement is to put the control back into the hands of the victim and hopefully have an effect on the length of the sentence imposed by the judge. Often it is an important part of the victim's recovery. Although we were not required to make this statement, I never doubted that I would seize the opportunity.

Several weeks before the sentencing, I began writing down all of my thoughts and feelings about Malone, describing the haunting memories that I still lived with. He seemed to have acquired a celebrity status in the weeks since he had pled guilty, and was often quoted in the media as professing his desire to help police locate another serial rapist. Since the media was closely following the events of this case, I knew that the statements of Malone's victims would reach many Detroit-area residents. It was one more opportunity for my voice to be heard and to get my message out. My hope now was that the other women that had fallen prey to Malone would feel the same, and together we would make a statement that would be heard loud and clear by our community.

TWENTY-FIVE

Survivors Speak Out

On the morning of March 21, 1988, Judge Lippitt's courtroom was once again filled to capacity. The detectives from each of the four Oakland County cities were present. Each victim was also there, with the exception of one woman that lived out of state. I had recently learned that her rape had occurred while visiting family in Michigan. The large group of people, including the media, added to the tension of an already stressful situation. It was about nine o'clock and most of us had been waiting for the sentencing to begin for at least a half hour. Feeling more nervous than I had anticipated, my attention was primarily focused on the victim impact statement that I gripped in my hands. It was my intention to speak directly to Judge Lippitt as I stated my position concerning Malone's sentence. However, I was worried that if I didn't read the words exactly as I had prepared them, I might forget half of what I wanted to say.

Deep in thought, my mom's nudge brought me back to the moment. When I looked up, Malone was entering the courtroom. His hands were shackled, and he was once again clutching his Bible, probably attempting to prove he was now a changed man.

Brian Zubel spoke first. "Your Honor, this is the date and time scheduled for sentencing in these matters and pursuant to MCL 780.765. There are, I believe, three victims with respect to these matters that wish to make victim impact statements at this time."

Judge Lippitt responded, "All right. Have them come forward."

Brian then called the victim from Oak Park to the front of the courtroom.

She looked nervous, yet when she spoke, her voice was strong and confident. Silently, I prayed for her. "Your Honor, I would like to address for the court the effects and the devastation of this crime on my life. I used to feel that I was an independent, competent, and tranquil person. As a result of this sexual assault, I feel like I have been diminished as a person in worth and self-esteem. As a result of these assaults and rape, I have been greatly shaken. I've had a persistent sense of helplessness, a feeling of lack of control over my life. On many days I have felt overwhelmed and unable to cope." Her words could easily have been mine.

She continued with her description of her fear and how she had lost her sense of security. As she neared the end of her statement, I listened intently as she described familiar feelings. "The rape and the assault are never completely out of my mind. I feel a lack of wholeness as a person. A part of me has been lost. I no longer have a sense of peace of mind. I yearn to be the person that I was before, with a sense of joy, with a sense of pleasure, with a sense of freedom and enthusiasm in my life, and I feel that has been taken away from me by this criminal. I fear that I will not be able to recover fully and I will not be able to be the person I was before." After concluding her statement, she walked slowly back to her seat.

Her words validated my own sense of loss that accompanied the sexual assault.

Without hesitation, the woman from Ferndale approached the front of the courtroom. In her eyes, I saw strength and determination. The courtroom was silent as she spoke. "The media has portrayed him as somewhat of a celebrity and the rapes are secondary. The real seriousness of the crimes he has committed has gone virtually unnoticed." Many people in the courtroom were nodding their heads, including myself. "I'll never be the same person I was before he broke into my home and attacked me. The fact that he stalked me for maybe weeks prior to that night is a scary thought. Knowing that someone was watching me, following me, without my knowledge, still makes me very uneasy. But the real fear was the fear of death. Try to imagine sleeping, then all of the sudden there's a hand on your mouth and a body on top of you and a strange voice saying, 'Don't scream.' Then try to imagine having your clothes cut off with a knife. I was naked, blindfolded, my hands and my feet tied with telephone cords, and I was left on my bed, not knowing if he was going to kill me or not. I couldn't see him, but I could hear him. Before, during, and after he raped me, I lay there waiting for death. Would a knife stab me or hands around my neck choke me? When he finally left without killing me, I almost wished he had, but I have come to realize that while he did take so much from me, I would never let him have my spirit." Malone's Ferndale victim had the undivided attention of every person in that courtroom. Her words were deeply moving, and the only dry eyes in the crowd belonged to Marc Malone.

Listening to this courageous woman made me realize that Malone had underestimated his victims. Although his intention was to prey on the defenseless, weak, and vulnerable, he had actually chosen women with an inner strength that could survive in the worst of situations. *Did this strength exist before each of us became his victims? Or has it developed within us during the difficult months that followed the sexual assaults?*

The courtroom remained hushed as the woman from Ferndale read her concluding remarks. "Malone is a very dangerous person and cannot be allowed to live freely in a society where he has to choose between right and wrong, because I truly believe he is unable to make the right choice."

Through my own tears, I could see others wiping their eyes. The impact of her words continued to linger in my own mind, and I remember being so proud of this woman who was able to touch the hearts of so many people. Everyone watched her as she picked up her papers and quickly turned away from the podium where she had been standing. As she returned to her seat, I looked toward Brian Zubel for some instruction. He looked at me and nodded his head. It was my turn.

Feeling light-headed and shaky, I steadied myself against the seat in front of me. Slowly, I walked towards the podium that faced Judge Lippitt, tightly gripping the paper I was holding. Glancing down at my statement, I attempted to read it, although my trembling hands made it difficult to focus on the words. Trying to calm myself, I closed my eyes and took a deep breath.

Putting down my speech, I spoke directly from my heart. At first, my thoughts were delivered in halting sentences, often starting my next thought before fully finishing the first one. All of the anger that I had stored inside of me came spilling out and I wasn't holding anything back. Speaking directly to the judge, I tried to discredit the media's portrayal of Malone as a remorseful man who had suddenly found God. "I couldn't believe that another human being could do this to me, and all of a sudden rape wasn't just something you read about in the papers, but I realized it actually happens to real people. His attempts that I read about to apologize in the newspapers turned my stomach. I can't believe that a person who watched me beg for my life and still didn't stop could suddenly be sorry for what he did . . . and his Bible doesn't fool me either!"

It was not my intent to react in an explosive manner, but it happened. Angry and defiant, I was not ready to believe that he had suddenly become virtuous. Every time he appeared in public, he was clutching a Bible. It seemed as though he was using God as a means of receiving a more lenient sentence from the court. He had expressed remorse and apologized during a previous interview. *How can a person be capable of tremendous cruelty one moment and then claim to be a Christian the next?* The thought of God forgiving him made me angry. My anger continued to escalate, and it was impossible to contain the words that I had held back for so long.

"I understand that he apologized to some of his other victims after he raped them. What makes these apologies any different than the ones before? He still continued to rape others. Marc Malone, himself, is responsible for every rape that he committed and nobody else. None of his phony apologies or blaming others can erase the damage that he's done to his victims and their families!"

I wasn't sure if I was making sense to those who were listening in the courtroom that day, but it didn't seem to matter. It felt good to say publicly that I could see right through Malone's ridiculous charade and know that he was listening. In an attempt to tell the Court about the devastating effect of rape on its victims, I described what life was like for me after surviving such an ordeal. "He took away my sense of security, all of my independence. I had to depend on friends and family to even walk in the house. You don't even have peace of mind when you're sleeping because the nightmares take over then, and you keep reliving that experience over and over again. I have no idea how I would cope if he was to be released from prison soon, and to know that he was walking around the streets again—I guess the best way I can describe how I feel each time I walk into my house is to compare it to walking down a dark alley in the middle of the city alone at night—I feel like that every time I walk in my house. Malone didn't just rape once on the spur of the moment. His actions were well planned and he did it more than once, and for this reason I ask you to please do everything you can to keep Marc Malone from ruining any more lives. Thank you."

I could feel Marc Malone's stare as I finished my statement. Finally at peace, I picked up the papers on which I had prepared my statement and walked back to my seat. Each victim who spoke had done all she could to help both the judge and the public understand the violent and devastating effect of sexual assault on the human soul. Now all we could do was wait for the judge to hand down a sentence, accept it, and go on with our lives.

"Does the prosecution have anything further to say?" Judge Lippitt asked.

"No, Your Honor," Brian answered.

The defense, though, did have an issue to discuss, and Malone was briefly excused from the courtroom. Judge Lippitt returned to his chambers, leaving the rest of us to speak among ourselves. We were all eager to hear the sentence Malone would be given. Twenty minutes would pass before Malone finally returned to the room. Judge Lippitt began questioning him again. "All right. Mr. Malone, do you wish to say anything before the court passes sentence?"

Malone stammered and appeared unsteady as he stood to give his response. "Yes, Your Honor. I would hope at this time to apologize to the victims and I know that there's not much more that words can say about . . . I'm very sorry that I became the person that I did, and that you became a person that was a part of my sickness. All I can hope and pray is that . . . that you can find some forgiveness and eventually you can find some feeling that will make your life get back to normal. I have absolutely no remorse—absolutely no, excuse me, no animosity and have no—will never have any consideration of having any kind of revengeful or any kind of violent responses ever in the future toward you and I hope you don't feel that I would be considered to do this again."

Malone was sobbing now, and stumbling over many of his words, however he still continued speaking. "I do need a lot of help and one of the things that I have found that's helped me a lot is the Bible and I'm becoming a little more of a Christian. I think that . . . I think that I have some positive qualities about myself and I hope that the court will look at that as a possibility of being able to be rehabilitated."

I would like to say that his proclamation that he was "becoming a little more of a Christian" helped me in my ability to forgive him. I would like to say that it caused me to pray for him and ask for the intervention of Jesus on his behalf. It didn't. I doubted his sincerity, and I was not finished being angry.

Malone continued speaking. "I think that the press had a lot of sensationalistic reporting on my case. I hope that your consideration of my incarceration, and hopefully my therapy, will be based on some of the professional reports as compared to the press, and that I think that I know I should definitely be incarcerated for a lengthy period of time but I do feel that I have the ability to control this and I hope that . . . I hope that the court will please give me the chance ten years down the line or whatever. I need a lot of help, Your Honor, and I just pray that you would have some mercy to give me a chance to be a more productive person in society instead of a burden on it the rest of my life." He paused for a moment and then concluded his statement. "Again, I would like to apologize to my victims and I pray that through your prayers and my prayers we can move on in our lives and I am deeply sorry. I apologize. That's all."

Judge Lippitt did not hesitate with his response. "All right. The court noted a few weeks ago in another sentence that attracted public attention and media attention that the judge doesn't win any awards in his sentencing, simply because the judge must consider and balance conflicting rights. The rights of the victim, the rights of society, and the rights of the defendant. The victims are hurt and they're angry and right-fully so, and there is no place in their hearts or their minds for any consideration of the defendant's professed illness or his previous background and reputation in the community. The defendant, on the other hand, is a person who by his course of conduct, although he today states that he has a considerable amount of remorse, has demonstrated that he is an extreme danger to the community and that must, of course, be taken into consideration in any sentence that the court metes out. These kinds of crimes are perplexing to the Court. They're even perplexing to behavioral scientists, who are supposed to know about this kind of behavior. It's hard for the court to imagine the fear and outrage that the victims have toward you Mr. Malone. I note that the criminologist, who was retained by you, has suggested that you can be rehabilitated, but he indicates that it will take a number of years in order to accomplish that goal. He states that it would be meaningless if you were simply warehoused in prison. He may be correct in that observation. It may be meaningless insofar as you're personally concerned, but I don't think it would be meaningless insofar as the victims are concerned, and perhaps not as far as society in general is concerned.

My obligation today is to recognize the seriousness of the crimes, to make certain that you are, in effect, warehoused so as to protect other women who may find themselves in like or similar circumstances and lastly, if possible, to provide some method for your rehabilitation if that is at all possible.

I have taken everything into consideration including the many, many letters that I have received on your behalf indicating that when you were a young man and into adulthood that you had a fine reputation in the community. I have also taken the letters of the detectives in charge of the cases into consideration as well as the statements of the victims and the statements of your attorneys."

Judge Lippitt began sifting through the papers in front of him, and it was obvious that he was preparing to read Malone's sentence. I held my breath. "All right, Mr. Malone. For your conviction of first-degree criminal sexual conduct on file number [file number], it's the sentence of the court that you be committed to the Michigan Department of Corrections for life imprisonment and that you be given credit for 254 days already served."

A quiet chorus of cheers erupted from the courtroom. Could I have heard the judge right? Was Malone just given a life sentence for the crime committed against me? Quickly I turned toward Marc Malone. The look on his face was one of complete shock. He then lowered his head and hid his face in his hands.

Many people were hugging each other and holding hands as the sentence was being read. The reporters were writing feverishly, attempting to gather all of the details. The judge then continued imposing sentences for the rapes of the remaining Oakland County women. "For your conviction of criminal sexual conduct in the second degree on [file number], the maximum sentence being fifteen years, it is the sentence of this court that you be committed to the Michigan Department of Corrections to serve a minimum term of not less than ten years, and a maximum term of not more than fifteen years."

The amount of prison time given for a second-degree offense was much less than that given for a first-degree offense. If no penetration was involved, Michigan law apparently limited the amount of time that can be served to fifteen years.

Judge Lippitt continued speaking. "Now there are three other cases to deal with in which you were convicted of first-degree criminal sexual conduct." He listed the file numbers of those three cases.

"On those three cases, Mr. Malone, it's the sentence of this court that you be committed to the Michigan Department of Corrections to serve a minimum term of not less than thirty-five years, and a maximum term of not more than a hundred years, and that you be given credit for 254 days as to each case. It is my duty to advise you, you have a right to appeal these convictions and sentences to a higher court. If you wish to do so, you must advise the court within fifty-six days of today. If you do, and we determine you are financially unable to hire a lawyer to appeal and you sign the form we are about to give you, we'll appoint a lawyer for you and furnish him the necessary transcript."

Mr. Larkins, spoke. "Your Honor, may the record indicate that I am tendering to Mr. Malone his appellate rights form."

"Thank you," the judge responded.

Brian Zubel then spoke and concluded the sentencing. "Thank you, Your Honor."

As we left the courtroom that morning, everyone around me seemed to be smiling. Malone would spend the majority, if not the rest, of his life behind bars. The victims, their families, the detectives, and even the people from the media seemed to be thrilled with the judge's decision. We were all hugging, tears of joy forming in many eyes. Detective Earnshaw remarked that it was the first time he had seen me smile.

I was overwhelmed with relief and gratitude. Most rapists are never caught, let alone prosecuted and given a life sentence. Police officers, detectives, forensic specialists, prosecutors, advocates, victims, and family members had united to end a vicious crime spree, and to make a strong statement to the public: Rape is a violent act that has devastating effects on its victims, and perpetrators will be dealt with severely. As victims, we refuse to keep silent and we speak openly about our experience without embarrassment. Shame and guilt belong only to the rapist.

At ten forty-five, it was too late for breakfast, and too early for lunch. Still, Judy invited each of the victims and the detectives involved in the case to a local restaurant for a bite to eat. She thought that it would be the perfect opportunity for us to get to know each other and share our thoughts in a more relaxed setting. Unfortunately, Detective Anger from Berkley was unable to attend, as was Detective Earnshaw. He had to hurry back to the Royal Oak police department. Disappointed that he wouldn't be joining us, I stood in the courthouse corridor trying to think of the right words to express my appreciation for his help and the patience he had shown me. More than likely, I would see Judy again while helping out at HAVEN, but I was unsure about Detective Earnshaw. He was the most difficult one to let go. Tears welling up in my eyes, about all I could manage was "Thank you."

TWENTY-SIX

STRENGTH IN NUMBERS

At the restaurant, the women from Oak Park and Ferndale were there, along with several of their family members. Judy, Detective Timmons, and Detective Raymond from Ferndale were seated near each other along one side of the table. I sat in between my mom and Judy.

After everyone spent several minutes looking at the menus, Judy broke the silence. "You all did a spectacular job with your victim impact statements. Each one of you chose a different way to deliver your message, and together you were very effective. Everyone in that courtroom was in awe of the strength and courage that each of you showed."

We could always count on Judy to lift our spirits and help us feel good about ourselves. She was able to convince a group of women who lived in constant fear that they were the most courageous women on earth. Mary Timmons added her own words of praise. Like Judy, her presence and her encouragement during the trial and throughout the entire legal process inspired us to keep going, and made us believe that we would eventually persevere. Now, all of us seemed to relax, and it became easier to start conversations with the other victims. This was the first time that I was given the chance to speak freely with any of these women.

One of the women shared her thoughts during the assault. She described how she had asked her assailant to get her a glass of water, thinking that he would leave his fingerprints on the glass as evidence for the police. Malone did get her the water, although no fingerprints were found. I listened to her story in amazement. *How was she able to think clearly enough to attempt to trick him into leaving his fingerprints?* I could only lie there hysterical, preparing myself to die. I admired her for being able to think rationally and calmly in the middle of a heart-stopping nightmare.

Another victim depicted the battle she had waged against the attorneys and the legal system during the planning and scheduling of the trial. She was the one who had defended the rights of each victim by attempting to reduce the number of times we would need to testify against Malone in court. This was something I would never have thought to do. The legal process was intimidating, and I was uncomfortable questioning the methods of the attorneys.

All of the victims expressed how grateful they were for the support of their families and the assistance they received from the detectives.

For some of us, faith played an important role in recovery. The woman from Ferndale had mentioned praying several times in her statement.

During one of the conversations, we questioned what provoked the attacks against us. Although some rapists might look for a specific physical characteristic, we ranged in age from about twenty to about fifty and were very different in our physical appearances. We discussed if how we dressed had any bearing on Malone choosing us. It didn't. At home, I wore a heavy bathrobe that covered me from my neck to my ankles. The morning I was raped, I was wearing sweats. In one interview, Malone had advised women to keep their blinds closed at night, as if opening windows and blinds on a hot, summer night was an invitation to be raped! In truth, Malone was a peeping Tom, and he chose us because we were easy targets—his intent being to control and conquer.

The connection that I felt with these women went beyond sharing a similar experience. We felt the same pain, had similar fears, and suffered the same losses. Our lives had changed in ways that were emotionally draining and intolerable. We were angry and unforgiving. Being with Malone's other victims was almost like looking into a mirror, and I was encouraged by what I saw! Staring back at me were women who had once believed that everything they had valued was lost, yet they found the strength to bounce back and rebuild their lives. Early in my own recovery, I had focused on my weaknesses and completely overlooked my accomplishments and strengths. Yet, friends had described me as being strong and resilient. It wasn't until I saw the strengths of these other women that I began to recognize them in myself. I sensed within all of us a renewed strength and appreciation for life. After facing our own mortality, we understood that just waking up in the morning was something to celebrate and be thankful for.

When I think of these women today, it is not their suffering that is foremost in my thoughts. Rather, I remember the courageous and determined spirit that emerged from each of them during their statements. In a way, I wanted to cling to them because I was worried that when we went our separate ways, I would lose the strength I had found in being with them. In the same way that I had felt that the police officers, detectives, and my HAVEN friends were intentionally put in my life, my heart was telling me that these other victims were a part of the support system that was provided to me by God. Our meeting gave me a sense of closure I might never have achieved if I hadn't talked with Malone's other victims.

After we had been talking for almost an hour, I noticed that the people in the booth near us were standing up to leave. Since I was not facing them directly, I paid little attention to what they looked like.

It wasn't until several minutes later that Judy leaned toward me and quietly said, "Those were his parents."

"Whose parents?" I asked.

"Marc Malone's mom and dad were sitting at that table over there having lunch. They just left."

Judy's words stunned me! We had been sitting in this booth talking openly about the devastation Malone had caused in our lives, and his parents were at the next table! *Could they have heard what we said? Certainly, they must have recognized us.* Admittedly, I had paid little attention to them in the courtroom. *Were they there during the sentencing, listening to each of their son's victims describe the torture he had put them through? How long have they been in the restaurant, subjecting themselves to our discussion about their son?*

TWENTY-SEVEN

THE MONSTER HAS A MOM

I never believed that Malone's parents were in any way responsible for his actions, nor did I find fault with them for supporting their son. According to the newspaper articles, his parents had recognized that their son had a problem and had tried to get him help. I had never really thought about them or the pain their son had caused them.

Thoughts of their plight lingered in my mind throughout the rest of our meal and on the days that followed. Malone had pled guilty, and forensic evidence confirmed it, so there was no question that he had committed the crimes. His parents knew he was responsible for our rapes, and still they remained by his side. I assumed they were strong people who supported and loved their son unconditionally. They weren't hiding from the truth but accepting it, and doing the best they could to move on with their lives.

These thoughts helped me realize that this man who had hurt so many people was loved by his family and by God. This thought bothered me. It made him seem like more of a human being and less of a monster. *If he was raised in a good family, what caused him to develop an obsession for inflicting pain on others?*

When interviews of Malone's parents and friends began appearing in newspapers, they portrayed him as an ambitious and gentle man who changed after his grandfather died. They described him as a "lost soul." These articles only fueled my anger. Countless people experience the loss of a grandparent—it seemed like a poor excuse for his violent, deviant behavior. These attempts to humanize Malone in the media did not diminish the hatred I felt toward him.

The idea of forgiving him for what he had done never entered my mind. We forgive friends and family members—people that we care about and love. My perpetrator was a monster. He was evil—a demon whose only purpose in life was to hurt others.

I have often heard people say that forgiveness is something we do for ourselves. As far as I was concerned, I had nothing to gain from it. I thought that I was doing just fine holding onto my anger and didn't see any reason to even consider forgiving my attacker. *Certainly Jesus wasn't thinking of rapists when he told us to forgive our enemies.* What Malone did to me and the other women was unforgivable.

What I didn't realize then was that the hatred and anger that I was clinging to was turning me into the same type of person that he was. Like him, I believed that someone else's suffering would alleviate my own. I perceived my anger as a way of regaining control in my life, but the longer it continued, the more it controlled me. At times it was all-consuming, affecting my mood and my attitude towards life. During the court proceedings, I saw this anger as a positive change—much better than the fear I had been living with.

Apparently, God thought differently and decided that it was time to intervene. He chose Marc Malone's parents to deliver the message.

When Judy invited us to lunch the morning of the sentencing, we had numerous restaurants to choose from in the area. *How is it that Malone's parents and his victims chose the same place? Is it a coincidence that we were seated at tables next to each other?* It occurred to me that this meeting was more than just a simple coincidence. It was an experience that would forever change the way I looked at my assailant. *The monster has a mom! He is somebody's son, brother, and friend. He is loved.* These new insights brought about a profound change within me. The grip I held on my anger relaxed. This was the first step in my journey towards the forgiveness of my assailant, a journey that would continue for many more years.

PART TWO

CHANGED FOREVER

After the trial, I moved on with my life. I followed my dreams, changed jobs, married, and became a mother. Twenty years have passed and I am happy, yet I have never forgotten those thirty minutes that changed my life forever. When my illusions of a problem-free existence were shattered by the assault, I believed that the rest of my life was ruined. Instead, I discovered that it was the birth of a new life—a life that began with more questions than answers, more suffering than joy—but a life that ultimately led to a deeper faith. My life has evolved in ways I could never have imagined as a result of being raped and the events that followed. I never want to forget the people that I met, the love that I felt, and the lessons that I learned throughout the many years of healing. This part of my book is my attempt to give meaning to my suffering. It is about the questions that I asked and some of the answers that time, faith, and reflections have given me as I have healed.

TWENTY-EIGHT

THE MYSTERY OF SUFFERING— WHY ME?

hy me? Though I never said the words aloud, it was a question that I have pondered repeatedly since that unfortunate morning. It's not that I thought the attack should have happened to someone else, but that I wondered if there was a reason that I was selected as Malone's victim. More specifically, *was it God's will that I was chosen or was I randomly selected?*

Often, the suffering I have experienced in my life was a consequence of my own selfish or irresponsible choices; therefore I deserved it. At other times, my suffering was caused by the loss of something or someone that was important to me. It was unavoidable and nobody's fault. The rape, however, was the result of someone else's deliberate, unprovoked actions. I developed a need to find a rational explanation for the reason God allows us to experience great pain.

When I experience tragedy in my life, am I being punished by God for something I did? Is God unhappy with me because of the mistakes I made in my life? Was I chosen because of my lack of faith? Did God choose not to help? Or is he not powerful enough to stop my intruder?

The concept of free will had helped me understand why God did not intervene during the rape. I was taught that when God created man, He gave us the freedom to make our own choices. It is a gift that is given out of love, to each of us, so that we are free to choose love. God doesn't police the world or demand that we do what is honorable. If He did, the love we give and receive would have no value. It would be forced and meaningless. However, we are also free to make choices that are destructive. Although God discourages us from living this way, He won't stop us. Therefore God did not intercede when Malone attacked me. This explains why God didn't stop the rape from happening.

But why does God allow suffering to exist? Does it have a purpose? Perhaps pain and suffering exist to teach us what's important in life? Negative experiences can certainly help me to appreciate the simple, day-to-day blessings. Yet, I wondered if the tragedies that happen are individually chosen by God to guide us toward Him and the type of life He wants for us. *Is He helping us to rearrange our priorities in order to find true happiness?*

Even so, it still bothered me to think that my misfortune was designed specifically for me. *How can a loving God inflict pain and suffering on one of His children intentionally?* Of course, I have no way of knowing for certain, but I'm reasonably confident that God never wills for other human beings to act cruelly. Thus, I decided my intruder's actions could not have been initiated by God. However, I do believe that God took advantage of my tragic situation, and used it to show me both His power and my own potential.

Although I did not get a definite answer to the "Why me?" question, it no longer matters. In my search for the truth, I came to know God. My prayer changed. It became honest and from the heart. Although I had been happy before the rape, I never knew what I was missing, and I began to crave a relationship with God.

As the days and weeks passed, my attitude and the questions I was asking began to change. Instead of asking, "Why me? Why this? Why now?" my questions changed to "What now? What have I learned? What can I do with this?" I realized that I had the choice of either wasting my suffering or using it. When I used it, it had purpose.

I don't believe that suffering is good or that God wants us to suffer. However, I do know that God uses moments of crisis to barge into our lives. Even if He seems to remain hidden for much of the time, tragedies and stressful situations are when I hear His answers most clearly—when I feel His presence. When I suffered, it was a calling. The answer to "What now?" became obvious to me: It was an invitation to share my experience and my faith.

All of us will experience much suffering during our lives. Suffering will always remain a mystery and we never *get over* things like the illness or the death of people we love and need, or the violation of our bodies and our spirits. The memories of our tragedies remain forever, but a greater appreciation for God and life can begin to overshadow the loss.

Upon reflection, I've concluded there are three things that contributed to my healing most. *Gratitude, God's Grace,* and *Forgiveness* gave me the strength I needed to continue my journey. They provided me with answers to many of my troubling questions.

TWENTY-NINE

GRATITUDE

Early in my healing process, I recognized that God was using the people around me to answer my prayers, ease my fears, and help me to trust again. I began to notice and appreciate the goodness that existed in others. As time went on, I became overwhelmed by the compassion that was shown to me, sometimes by people I had only recently met.

My family helped me to feel safe by installing security devices in my house and by staying with me so I wouldn't be home alone. My mom and aunt accompanied me to court. My friends, including my roommate, listened to me monologue my concerns. A woman I had never met helped me to remember what it was like to be independent by providing a place for me to stay in California. A coworker that I had known for less than a year accompanied me in my search for a dog to regain a sense of security. A professor I had only briefly met trusted me to speak at a local university about the haunting effects of rape on its victims, thus giving me renewed self-confidence and the opportunity to make a difference. A victim's advocate and a detective held my hand throughout my difficult journey through the criminal justice system.

At times, it was a brief encounter with someone that gave me strength. A friendly smile gave me great courage. A few kind words can lift a person's spirits and possibly change their life. Any person that interacts with victims of sexual assault has within them the power to help heal.

In the process of writing this book, I wondered if those who helped me realized how deeply they had influenced my life. Suddenly, it became important to let each of them know that I still remember them and am grateful for their support. However, twenty years had passed since I had spoken to many of them. *Will they remember me or the rape case that they had worked on? How will I find them?*

I needed to try. Determined, I set out to let them know that they had made a difference in my life, and probably the lives of many others. Perhaps thanking them now could give me the sense of closure that I still longed for. Originally, I believed that closure would involve an apology or some sort of explanation from Malone. As I contacted those special individuals, I came to realize that an apology was no longer necessary. I found closure in showing my gratitude for the kindness that was given to me, and in letting my angels know the impact of their compassion and devotion.

I began calling and visiting the different police stations and court-houses located in the cities affected by the twenty-year-old crime. Surprisingly, it didn't take long for me to get in touch with almost all of the men and women that had assisted me years earlier. Some were still working while others had retired, but gradually I was able to meet each one of them personally. Detectives, judges, police officers, an attorney, and a victim's advocate not only allowed me to enter their lives again, but were eager to talk to me. Although my intention was simply to show my appreciation for all they had done, I underestimated the power of the words "Thank you." It was as much a joy for me to say the words as it was for them to hear them. How delighted God must be when we remember to include those two words in our prayers!

Through the years, I often wondered whether the benevolence I had perceived in these friends was real or imagined. After reuniting with each of them, I knew that their kindness and compassion had been authentic and genuine, and even more evident now than it was twenty years ago. Their memories of this case were better than I had hoped, and I gained a new, unexpected understanding of the events that followed the rape. These people were special because of their willingness to involve their hearts in their work. They didn't hesitate to empathize with the victims they encountered and were dedicated to easing their suffering.

After meeting with these heroes from my past, I gained a clearer picture of God's influence in my recovery.

Mike Strubel, the first police officer to respond on the day of the rape, explained that on that particular morning he had been assigned to traffic detail. It was only because his fellow officers were busy attending to other calls that he was summoned to my house. Talking with him, I suddenly felt as though God had hand-picked the person who would be instrumental in determining my attitude throughout my recovery.

In a recent conversation with Detective Fred Earnshaw, I described the terror I felt while living in my Royal Oak house after I was raped but before Malone was caught. The detective smiled warmly and said, "We watched your house regularly after the break-in. There was often an unmarked police car parked on your street, keeping an eye on you and your roommate. We were determined to keep him from ever hurting you again."

I was shocked! During those early months, I was constantly looking over my shoulder. *How is it possible that I was unaware of someone watching over and protecting Joanne and me?* It is a great reminder that even though we don't always see our guardians, it doesn't mean that they aren't near. Each time I tried to thank Detective Earnshaw, he responded with the phrase, "I'm just doing my job." The detectives I had come to know went above and beyond "just doing their jobs." They didn't hesitate to open their hearts and empathize with the victims they encountered, and it was important to them to help each victim return to a normal life.

My only regret is that I was unable to locate Malone's other victims to let them know the impact they had on me. They were intelligent, courageous women whose presence helped me to endure the court proceedings and face my attacker. I will never forget them and hope that they, too, have been blessed in their lives as I have been in mine.

For me, the people that helped the most were the ones that gave me the opportunity to talk. Although this might not be true of all victims, I needed to express my fears verbally. It was a way for me to organize my thoughts and release some tension. Not only did they listen, but they weren't afraid to ask questions. Some, like Ike McKinnon, Mary Timmons, and Judy from

HAVEN, recognized the need that I had to give a purpose to my suffering, and gave me the opportunity to educate others about rape and its affect on its victims, thus facilitating my healing. After Malone's sentencing, I began volunteering with HAVEN's Speaker's Bureau. Although I had little experience speaking in front of groups, I found myself talking to men and women who were in some way involved with victims of violent crimes. Speaking publicly was often downright terrifying. Sometimes I participated on panels with other victims of violent crimes. Our purpose was to speak to the news media, sharing our thoughts and feelings about the coverage of our stories. This gave me the opportunity to make a difference in the lives and attitudes of society in general. Whether it involved the education of people who initially responded to victims, giving hope to other victims, or changing the attitudes of families who blamed the victims for what had happened to them, it felt good to speak out.

The compassionate treatment I received had stimulated a desire within me to give back some of what had been given to me. It seemed that the best way to honor those who had helped me was to imitate them. They made a difference in my life, and I seized every opportunity to make a difference in the lives of others. God gave to me through others, and I hoped that I could give back to God through others.

THIRTY

GRACE

The first time in my life that I truly felt loved by God was during the rape. He felt my pain and terror, and helped to cushion it. He guided my thoughts toward memories of my family and loved ones, taking my mind off the disturbing actions of the rapist.

Later, I was reminded that Jesus repeatedly gave one command more than any other in scripture. He said, "Do not be afraid." I believe these are the same words He said to me as I lay on my living room floor, expecting to die. In the days that followed, the soft whisper of those words stayed with me. In His presence, there was nothing to fear, not even death.

Perhaps this calming sensation is the same one that is felt by others facing imminent death. I am acutely aware of news stories describing people who used their cell phones to call loved ones in the midst of catastrophic circumstances. They usually focused on telling family members how much they loved them, rather than expressing their fear of dying. It appeared that God had rushed to their side also, calming them and letting them know that they would be okay. *Did these people also recognize that God was with them, giving them the courage to face their own mortality?*

Afterwards, I began noticing His presence at other times. Another dimension had been added to my life, and God was at the center of it. I developed a burning desire to tell everyone about the miracles I was experiencing in my life and wanted everyone to feel my excitement and share my new awareness. Yet, in order to talk about the miracles, I had to talk about the rape. Both subjects had a tendency to make other people uncomfortable.

Gradually, I understood that my experience could be summed up in one word: *grace.* Initially, I thought grace was a blessing or a gift that God gives us when we need help. My experience has taught me that I had greatly underestimated the power and magnitude of God's grace. I learned that grace is the unmerited, unearned love God gives to every one of us. We belong to Him, and He will always provide us with what we need.

Sometimes, I think, it is easier to see this grace in others than it is to recognize it in ourselves. Often we look at other people who have suffered great adversity or loss and think, *How can they possibly function given all they have been through?* At times they appear to grow even stronger in the midst of horrible tragedies. God seems to give His Grace to individuals in their time of need. Observers are not given this special grace, and therefore can't fully comprehend how the injured person can cope.

When I witness this occurrence in others it is inspiring and I am in awe of God and His healing powers. Grace allows us to accept peacefully the tragedy that has occurred in our lives. Somehow we are given the ability to act rationally in an intolerable situation. It is an inner strength that helps us make sense out of senselessness. It is God's answer to our cries for help.

God seems to make his strongest appearances during the times we are most weak and vulnerable. Perhaps these are the times when we are more likely to invite him into our lives. While growing up and during my early adult years, I believed that if I asked for God's help in trivial matters that I would be bothering Him. I found it difficult to love or feel loved by a God I was afraid to talk to or call on for help. Yet, in the days that followed the rape, I felt His presence at times when I didn't call Him! *Is it possible that He wants me to ask for His help?* I now believe that he had been waiting patiently for me to call upon Him. I came to understand that my problems are never trivial to God because I am His daughter.

Even though I am aware that tragedy is not only possible but probable for all of us, I worry less about it. The certainty of suffering has taught me the importance of appreciating and enjoying today. Now I trust that when I need God's grace, it will come, and it is all that I will need.

THIRTY-ONE

FORGIVENESS

Immediately after the rape, my anger at Malone created an illusion of having power and provided protection against my emotional pain. I have since come to understand that my anger kept me chained to him, reminding me of my anguish.

Through my Catholic faith, I have been taught that I should forgive my enemies. But what does that mean, exactly? Does it mean that I should no longer think about the incident? That is impossible. Does it mean that I must release Malone from all responsibility for his actions? Surely he needs to be held accountable for his actions and live with the consequences.

Through the years, whenever I spoke with others about forgiving Malone, I was often met with skepticism. They assumed that forgiving him meant that I wanted him released from prison. Most people seemed to believe forgiveness was something you do only for the perpetrator's sake, a way of letting him off the hook for his crimes. It took years for me to realize that the person doing the forgiving actually benefits more.

It did require an effort on my part to choose to forgive him. Finding the desire within me to forgive him was difficult. It was something I needed God's help to do. It required a willingness to include Malone and his family in my prayers. In the book *Compassion*, spiritual writer Henri Nouwen illustrates the importance of praying for those who have hurt you. He says, "It is impossible to lift our enemies up in the presence of God and at the same time continue to hate them." Whenever I am tempted to cling to my anger, it helps me to remember this.

Previously, I found great pleasure in imagining the torment Malone would probably experience in prison. As the years passed, I noticed that I had lost my desire for Malone to hurt. Believing he was capable of raping again, I still wanted him locked up, but I was hopeful that he would find peace in his life. I could never forget what Malone had done to me and the other women, yet dwelling on those thoughts magnified the bitterness that I felt. The internal tension and anxiety had been poisoning me; however, it had no affect on Malone.

Memories of the horror and despair have a tendency to resurface throughout my life. Each time I feel that fear and connect it to him, I must choose to forgive him again. At first, it required a tremendous effort on my part to continue praying for him. Jesus gives us specific instructions on how to respond to people that hurt us. It says in scripture, "Love your enemy." Forgiving him was one thing, but *love* him? You've got to be kidding!

Then, one day, about ten years after the assault, I developed an even greater understanding of the meaning of love and forgiveness, and I realized that they are connected. I was married and had two small children. It had been a difficult week. My husband was traveling for his job, and I was trying to balance working part-time, taking care of the house, and looking after our children. On Friday of that particular week, I was feeling especially down, regretting some of the decisions I had made that day, and throughout my life. The younger of my two daughters had thrown several temper tantrums, and my patience was exhausted. Time after time, I raised my voice to my children and felt like the world's worst mother. When my husband came home from traveling that evening, I asked him to watch the kids while I spent some time alone.

My first thought was to go to the chapel at our church. When I arrived, it was empty. I found a seat near a window. The serene atmosphere touched me, and my emotions poured out as I spoke to God. I began weeping and pleading for forgiveness for all the mistakes I had made throughout my adult life. For one hour, I told God about everything that was bothering me. I calmed down significantly. Concluding my prayer, I tearfully asked God to forgive me. Then I picked up my jacket, rested my left hand on the chair next to me, and braced myself before standing up. I noticed that my hand was touching a booklet. Slowly, I read the words in large, bold letters printed across the top: "You Are Forgiven."

Astonished, I fell back into the chair. *Is this God's response to my plea?* The peaceful presence that I had felt during the rape and in the midst of the worrisome exam at work had returned. *If I can be loved and forgiven for the wrongs I have committed, I need to love and forgive others for their mistakes.*

I left the chapel that evening in a state of shock, never thinking to pick up the booklet and read the rest of the pages. In the days that followed, I returned, several times, but was never able to find it. Perhaps the message I had already been given was all that I needed.

Those three words were so powerful that they impacted the rest of my life. They changed my relationship with God and with others. It became clear to me that I had faults like everyone else, and that no one person was more or less forgivable than another. I became more tolerant. The words "you are forgiven" helped me realize that God loved me and was willing to forgive any mistakes that I make, without hesitation. There are no conditions attached. I only need to ask. Now I understood that I was expected to do the same for my enemies. That recognition put an end to any leftover anger that I still harbored towards Malone. The words from the Lord's Prayer—"Give us this day our daily bread, and forgive us our trespasses, as we forgive those who trespass against us"—suddenly made perfect sense, and I understood exactly what was expected of me.

Forgetting is not the same as forgiving. The seeds of forgiveness were given to me the day I realized Malone had parents. Yet it has taken twenty years to complete this part of the healing process.

Finally, I have a sense of what it means to love your enemy. To me, love means praying for my enemy and trusting that God will do what is best for him. It is hoping that God's grace and mercy will touch the life of the person who has hurt me.

This book is my contribution to witnessing God's love. It is a journey I will never forget. On Tuesday, January 16, 2007, at my request, a Mass was said for the man who raped me.

APPENDIX 1:
The Crime of Rape

According to RAINN (Rape, Abuse, and Incest National Network), a sexual assault occurs every two and a half minutes in America. One out of every six women has experienced either an attempted or completed rape in their lifetime. One out of every thirty-three men has been sexually assaulted. Over half of all sexual assaults go unreported.

If you become a victim of a sexual assault, there are a number of things to keep in mind immediately following the attack. Most importantly, find a safe place to go, away from the attacker. Know that it was not your fault, and begin taking steps to report the crime to the police by calling 911. Do not bathe or brush your teeth. Write down everything you can remember about the assault and the perpetrator. Forensic evidence will help with the future prosecution of the rapist. Ask for a rape kit exam at the hospital and if you suspect that you were drugged, request that a urine sample be collected. Many hospitals have SANE (sexual assault nurse examiners) nurses available that are specially trained. You are not committed to prosecuting if you later decide against it.

If you choose not to report a rape, it is important that you still get medical attention for your injuries. Even if you have no obvious signs of physical trauma, you might still be at risk for sexually transmitted diseases (STDs) and pregnancy. It is never too late to call for help.

It is important to remember that every sexual assault victim may have different reactions. Personal beliefs, whether or not the victim knew their attacker, the reaction of friends and family, the circumstances preceding the rape, and the age of the victim are just a few of the factors that may influence a person's response to the assault.

Frequently, a person has trouble functioning in the same way they did before the rape. Among the more common reactions to a sexual assault are the following:

- Intense feelings of fear and helplessness
- Feeling numb or dazed
- Difficulty remembering details of the rape
- Experiencing nightmares or flashbacks of the assault
- Intense anxiety
- Avoidance of people or places that are reminders of the assault
- Self blame
- Shock
- Feeling vulnerable and weak
- Humiliation and shame

These thoughts and feelings can be intense during the months immediately following the assault, and they may persist for a year or longer without treatment and counseling. Many rape victims turn to drugs and alcohol to relieve their stress.

Depression is a common psychological reaction to a sexual assault. Symptoms may include crying spells, changes in eating or sleeping habits, fatigue, excessive worry and anger, the inability to concentrate, and thoughts of suicide. When these symptoms last more than two weeks, it is a sign that it is more than just normal sadness.

If someone you love has been raped, you may also be experiencing intense and disturbing emotions. Anger is typical. You can be angry at the person who hurt your loved one and angry at the rape victim for putting herself in a dangerous situation. It is not uncommon to feel guilt or frustration over your inability to help the victim or her inability to recover. You might feel sadness over her losses or even believe that the rape brought shame upon your family. It is important that anyone close to the victim who is struggling with these feelings gets professional help.

On average, rapists are not the type of person we would expect. Again, according to RAINN, About 73 percent of rape victims know their assailant. According to the 1997 Sex Offenses and Offenders study, 52 percent of rapists are white. About 22 percent of rapists in prison say they are married and their average age is thirty-one at the time of their arrest.

There is no way to distinguish a rapist from any other person on the street because they don't dress a certain way or act unusual. They often give the appearance of being good family men and productive members of society. Many are well dressed and clean shaven—men with respectable jobs. However, they have serious psychological disorders and use sexual violence as a means of expressing power and anger. More often than not, they choose victims of their own race. They don't see their victims as human beings, but as unfeeling objects on which to vent their fury and frustrations. They are not deterred by any possible consequences for their actions.

To reduce your risk of being assaulted:

- Avoid isolated areas or being alone with someone you don't trust.
- Don't overload yourself with packages; it will make you vulnerable to an attack.
- Be aware of your surroundings, and don't put music headphones in both ears if you are alone. Pay attention to who is around you.
- Always carry money for cab fare and keep a charged cell phone with you.
- Walk with your head up and act like you have a purpose and a destination, even if you don't.

Trusting our instincts is usually our best defense. If you sense that your situation is unsafe, it probably is.

Appendix 2:
Resources

National Sexual Assault Hotline:

RAINN—Rape, Abuse, & Incest National Network
Website: www.rainn.org
Crisis Line: 1-800-656-HOPE

Michigan Coalition Against Domestic and Sexual Violence:

3893 Okemos Rd., Ste. B2
Okemos, MI 48864
Phone: 517-347-7000
Website: www.mcadsv.org

Michigan Sexual Assault Hotlines:

HAVEN—Help Against Violent Encounters Now (Pontiac)
Website: www.haven-oakland.org
County Served: Oakland
Crisis Line: 248-334-1274
Toll Free: 877-922-1274

Turning Point, Inc. (Mt. Clemens)
Website: www.turningpointinc.com
County Served: Macomb
Crisis Line: 586-463-6990

Detroit Police Department Rape Counseling Center (Detroit)
County Served: Wayne
Hotline: 313-833-1660

First Step (Plymouth)
Website: www.firststep-mi.org
County Served: Wayne
Crisis Line: 734-459-5900
Toll Free: 888-453-5900

Safe Horizons (Port Huron)
Website: www.safehorizonsmi.org
County Served: St. Clair
Crisis Line: 810-985-5538
Toll Free: 888-985-5538

YWCA—Domestic Assault/Sexual Assault Services (Flint)
County Served: Genesee
Crisis Line: 810-238-7233

MSU Sexual Assault Crisis Line (East Lansing)
County Served: Ingham
Crisis Line: 517-372-6666

Safe House Center (Ann Arbor)
Website: www.safehousecenter.org
County Served: Washtenaw
Crisis Line: 734-995-5444

YWCA West Central Michigan (Grand Rapids)
Website: www.ywcawcmi.org
County Served: Kent
Crisis Line: 616-776-7273

Bay Area Women's Center (Bay City)
Website: www.bayareawomenscenter.org
Counties Served: Bay, Arenac
Crisis Line: 989-686-4551
Toll Free: 800-834-2098

Underground Railroad, Inc. (Saginaw)
Website: www.undergroundrailroadinc.org
County Served: Saginaw
Crisis Line: 989-755-0411
Toll Free: 888-399-8385

Caring Alternatives (Monroe)
County Served: Monroe
Crisis Line: 734-243-6410

Women's Resource Center, Grand Traverse Area (Traverse City)
Website: www.womensresourcecenter.org
Counties Served: Grand Traverse, Leelanau, Antrim, Benzie,
  Kalkaska
Crisis Line: 231-941-1210
Toll Free: 800-554-4972

Aware, Inc. (Jackson)
County Served: Jackson
Crisis Line: 517-783-2861

Sexual Assault Services of Calhoun County (Battle Creek)
Counties Served: Branch, Barry, Eaton, Calhoun, Surrounding
Crisis Line: 888-383-2192

YWCA of Kalamazoo
Website: www.ywcakalamazoo.org
Counties Served: Kalamazoo
Crisis Line: 269-345-3036

Women's Center/Harbor House (Marquette)
Website: www.mcmqt.org/
Counties Served: Marquette, Alger
Crisis Line: 906-226-6611
Toll Free: 800-455-6611

Diane Peppler Resource Center (Sault Ste. Marie)
Counties Served: Chippewa, Luce, Mackinac
Crisis Line: 906-635-0566
Toll Free: 800-882-1515

Acknowledgments

All of us will experience tragedy during our lifetimes. Although it can be difficult to move past the suffering, it is during these times that God rushes to our side, often by sending other people to help us. These are the people I want to thank for saying yes when God asked them to help me. Some of them were there for me twenty years ago. Others came into my life more recently.

I am grateful to my family and friends for their support and patience throughout my recovery and during the writing of this book. Although I must have tested their patience, they never abandoned me. My dear friends, both from the past and the present, have inspired me to keep writing just by asking about the progress of my manuscript and showing an interest in my story. With patience, they listened to me say "It's almost done" over and over again for the last three years. Thank you Mom, Dad, Joanne, Sean, Bernadette, Lisa, Richard, Linda, Gerry, Jim, Renee, Becky, Trish, Donna, Michelle, Ann, Carol, Betty, Susan, Carole, and Pam.

To Mom, Dad, and Joanne, your courageous battles with cancer have inspired me throughout my writing, and I watched in awe as each of you persevered and never lost your ability to smile.

Thanks to Richard who said to me in the days following the rape, "You should write a book!" At the time I thought his idea was ridiculous, but he had planted a seed, and now, twenty years later, I have done exactly as he suggested.

To the family of Barbara Joyce, it was an honor to have met such a special woman.

I am grateful to Mike Struble, the first officer to speak to me on the morning of the rape, for laying the foundation for the attitude I would

183

carry with me from that day forward. Sexual assault is a horrific crime. I had every right to be angry and no reason to feel embarrassed or humiliated as a result of what happened to me.

Thank you to all of the detectives involved in the case against my rapist. Detectives Norman Raymond, Ray Anger, Mary Timmons, and Fred Earnshaw opened my eyes to the devotion and compassion that exists in so many law enforcement officials. I have developed a great appreciation for all the work they do, and all detectives now hold a special place in my heart.

Special thanks to Mary Timmons and Fred Earnshaw for taking the time to read my book, and for their insightful, professional comments.

Brian Zubel, the prosecuting attorney, treated me with great respect and compassion, always offering me an encouraging word. Although I had not talked to him for twenty years, he did not hesitate to give me whatever help I needed during the writing of this book.

Isaiah "Ike" McKinnon gave me a sense of self-worth and confidence. He taught me that I had something important to say, and that I had the ability to make a difference in the lives of others. He helped me to understand that my life and the suffering that I experienced could have a purpose and that it didn't need to be wasted.

Judy from HAVEN was responsible for teaching me that I was a strong and capable woman who would be able to recover from this tragic experience. I am grateful to everyone I met at HAVEN for helping me regain my confidence and to stop thinking of myself as a victim.

I am grateful to Fr. John Riccardo, the greatest teacher I have ever met, who inspired me throughout much of my writing and faith development. Thank you for taking the time to read my manuscript and for your candid suggestions.

Thanks to Sheri, who not only listened to me talk repeatedly about my book, but as a result of her suggestion, I was able to find the right publisher.

Thank you to my publisher, Marian Nelson, for the personal service and for giving me the opportunity to share my story, and to my editor, Jan Jones, who made the editing process both enjoyable and exciting.

A very special thank you to Tom Bruno, an author himself, for the time he spent helping me with my writing. When I told him that I wanted to write a book about my experience, he said, "Don't tell me, show me." I am grateful beyond words to Tom for his encouragement and professional help.

Without the support of my husband, Chris, I could never have finished this book. Thank you, Hon, for all the times you spent playing video games with the kids in order to give me time to write. To my children, Erin, Amy, and Adam, thank you for understanding when Mom needed time to work on her book. I love you all.

About the Author

Julie M. Frawley is a survivor of a sexual assault that occurred more than twenty years ago. It is her hope that by sharing her experience and the process of healing that followed, others will be inspired to overcome their own adversities. Frawley attended a program at HAVEN that trained her to interact with other victims of sexual assault and domestic violence. She has spoken publicly and participated on panels that discuss the affects that rape has on its victims. She lives in Michigan with her husband and three children.